D1349410

The Education of a Woman Golfer

The Education of a Woman Golfer

Nancy Lopez

with Peter Schwed

Pelham Books
London

First published in the United States of America by
Simon and Schuster
A Division of Gulf & Western Corporation
Simon & Schuster Building
Rockefeller Center
1230 Avenue of the Americas
New York
New York 10020
1979

First published in Great Britain by
Pelham Books Ltd
44 Bedford Square
London WC1B 3DU
1980

ISBN 0 7207 1272 6

Printed in Great Britain by
Hollen Street Press, Slough
and bound by
Hunter & Foulis Ltd, Edinburgh

*To my mother and my father
the two people who
made everything possible*

Acknowledgments

The Ladies Professional Golf Association was most generous in making available both factual material and a number of the photographs that appear in this book. Special thanks are due Chip Campbell and Ruffin Beckwith. The LPGA photographs are the ones on pages 42, 75, 78, 95, 96, 98, 101, 104, 105, 107, 108, 109, 111 (bottom), 112, 113, 114, 116, 117, and 118.

Nancy Platzer, who specializes in women's golf photography, took the pictures that appear on the frontispiece and on pages 58–59, 76, 97, 99, 100, 102, 106, 111 (top), 115, 119, 133, 135, 142, 144, 161, and 170.

Wide World Photos, Inc., supplied those on pages 25, 43, 48, 49, 62, 64, 88, 131, 132, 139, 145, 147, 156, 173, 175, 177, 178, and 182.

Lester C. Nehamkin took the one on page 21.

Bill Garlow, of the *Dayton Journal Herald*, shot the one on page 137.

The article and the accompanying photographs that are on pages 28–33 inclusive originally appeared in *Golf Digest* and are used here by the kind permission of that magazine.

Contents

Foreword

"Education is . . . hanging around until you've caught on."
ROBERT FROST

THE OFFICIAL RECORDS say that Nancy Marie Lopez was born in Torrance, California, on January 6, 1957, but I know better. The significant birth for me, and certainly as far as this book is concerned, took place on a fairway of the municipal golf course in Roswell, New Mexico, when I was eight years old. My golf education began at the same moment. It happened this way.

The family has moved to Roswell several years before, and both my father, Domingo, and my mother, Marina, were golfers. Dad was real good, while Mom was just a weekend-type woman golfer, but they both loved the game and each other and they played a lot together. I used to tag along and watch but then, on that certain big day, Dad pulled Mom's 4-wood out of her bag, handed it to me, and simply said, "Hit it. You just keep on hitting until you get that ball into the hole. Now stay just back of us, little one, but keep up too, because the people in back will be right close and we don't want you to get in the way or anything like that, you see?"

That was my first golf lesson and Dad has been my only real golf teacher ever since. I've never had a real golf lesson from a professional in my life, and the fact of the matter is that Dad's instructions in the years that followed were seldom very much more elaborate than that first one. Sometimes he would spot something in my swing that I usually did correctly, but wasn't doing right at that moment, and he'd tell me about it. But usually I just learned by watching him and other good players and that, combined with a blessedly lucky aptitude for the game, has always been very nearly everything I needed to achieve whatever my golf technique is today. Even I am not really sure exactly what that is: I simply do what seems to come naturally.

Well, returning to that day on the course at Roswell, which I really don't remember that well, Dad has told me that the whole thing immediately and unexpectedly became very complicated because, right away, my ball flew over my parents' heads and each time they went on ahead, and I waited to fall back of them, the same thing happened again and again. Apparently I hardly ever missed, but would just step up and swing and I kept knocking that one ball on the nose and down the fairway. It did slow things up for my folks and me to keep playing this sort of leapfrog pace, and my Dad was nervous about blocking the people in back of us, so once I had reached the green he would only allow me to take one putt with my mother's putter. He said "I'll give you that" on any putt I had left myself, and tell me to pick up my ball and hustle off the green. I would score for myself whatever number of strokes I'd taken up to where I was then lying on the green, but I didn't add anything for the conceded putt. That was logical, wasn't it? I scored the actual shots I had taken.

Also, I was teeing up every shot on the fairway, and I guess that's one good reason why my 4-woods soared so well and never beaned my dear parents. It was some time later that I learned the rules didn't allow that, and that you had to putt out and count every stroke. But that day I had a very gratifying score using my rules for the holes I played, considering that it was my very first time out. The big thing was that I was completely hooked on golf.

Maybe the even bigger thing was that so were Mom and Dad—hooked on golf *for me!* From that day on they encouraged me and did absolutely everything they could to let me expand toward becoming a real golfer. I'll tell you more about that in the chapter that follows. A golfer's education may begin by swinging a 4-wood at a teed-up golf ball and managing to hit it successfully, but a great many other things build on top of it, and some of them don't take place on the golf course or the practice tee.

My formal and traditional academic education was okay insofar as it went. I wasn't a bad student at all throughout

Mom and Dad and I seem to have decided not to have a formal family photograph taken in golf clothes.

the grade years and high school, knocking off quite a few A's, mostly B's, and only an occasional C. Math was my best subject, so I planned to major in Engineering when I got to college, and I did specialize in it through my freshman year at Tulsa University. It was hard going, though, so I changed to Business Administration as a sophomore. If I had stayed on at Tulsa for my junior year I think I would have switched again—this time to Basket Weaving.

But by that time, apart from the academic pressure, I'd been doing so well in amateur golf that taking the plunge into the professional game really was irresistible. Finally I would have the opportunity to make money and start repaying my parents for all the sacrifices they had made to get me to this point. So I dropped out of college and went on the LPGA tour, which is a whole other ball game from amateur golf and a scene that continued the education I really craved—my golfing education—far past any other way I could have spent the rest of my college years.

That, and what led up to it, is what this book is all about.

The
Education
of a
Woman
Golfer

Chapter 1

Teeing Off from the Rough

My Education in Economics and Sociology

TRADITIONALLY, golf has always been more of a game for the privileged than most other sports. Admittedly it's not polo. You don't have to own a string of polo ponies. And it's true that many of the great male golfers of the long ago past, like Gene Sarazen and Walter Hagen, emerged out of the caddie ranks. But today, on the whole, most good golfers have had backgrounds, sufficient wealth, or at least sufficient opportunity, so that they went to a school or a college with a good golf program, or they belonged to a country club, or something like that. Lee Trevino and Lee Elder are exceptions who come to mind, but there aren't too many top-notch golfers who once were caddies or who used the public courses. Baseball stars come up all the time from the sandlots. Football and basketball are such big sports in public schools and state colleges that the cream of the talent naturally comes to the top and turns into the stars of the professional games. Even so social a sport as tennis has been through the years can be played comparatively cheaply and easily on public courts all over the country, so that anyone has a pretty good chance to grow if he or she has the stuff.

But serious golf can be really expensive. Equipment costs a lot, joining a private club (assuming you rate an invitation to join!) costs even more, and between travel and the inevitable expenses involved on every round of golf, only the fairly well-to-do are likely to be able to play and practice regularly enough so that a possible career in golf is practical. So even though Dad and Mom were thrilled at the way I hit a golf ball instinctively at the age of eight, there were a couple of natural obstacles in the way if their heartwarming excitement and confidence in my potential was ever going to come to anything.

Sufficient money was the first of the two obstacles. My Dad, Domingo (or "Sunday" as many friends call him, that being the literal translation of his name), owned and ran a good auto-body repair shop in Roswell. The money he made from that had supported us very pleasantly in our little two-bedroom, one-bath house, which is what it was then. Later Dad built a den and a dining room and another bedroom onto it, but back then we lived less luxuriously. Dad also had always managed to take care of all the other things that he now began to think of as incidentals: food, taxes, utilities, medical bills, and that sort of unexciting stuff. The trouble was that there wasn't much money left over for what he and Mom now considered our prime necessity—giving their child every chance to develop her golfing skills.

My mother made the first move. She had never been anything more than an enthusiastic duffer, and she now said that even with greens fees on our municipal course as inexpensive as they were, three golfers in the family added up to one too many. Domingo and Nancy were the real golfers anyway. Apart from that, she used the excuse that a recent gallbladder operation she had undergone probably made it wise for her to give up the game. So that is what she did, turning over all her clubs to me.

The fact is that although she was never very good at it, my mother loved golf and, seeing what she did for me in later years, it's my bet that her explanation about her gallbladder was just so I wouldn't feel guilty about her sacrifice. It's true that, between being somewhat overweight and diabetic, she was not in the best of health, but I think the real thing was that she always had me and my sister, Delma, much more in her mind than herself. For instance in my case, once I started to do well as an amateur, she would never let me wash the dishes again because she insisted that the hot water would soften my hands and so harm my swing. Then she told Dad that she didn't want a better house when he offered to get us one, and she turned down his suggestions that we get several other things that could have made her household work easier, such as a washing machine and a dishwasher. Dad could have afforded such expenditures, but not if $100 a month was going to be put aside regularly like clockwork to enable me to travel and play in tournaments and find out if I was good enough ever to be a professional. Mom and Dad were really a team in caring for their children's concerns, and by this time I was the lone recipient of their solicitous and loving attention. Delma, my elder sister by a dozen years, had married when she was sixteen and had gone off to live in California with her husband, Bernie Guevara, so since I was four I had been the equivalent of an only child. (I *hated* it when Delma left, and I still remember how, as she packed her clothes to go, I ran over and took each thing out of her suitcase a moment after she had carefully put it in!) Now Mom and Dad both kept doing without things for my ben-

My first and only coach

efit alone. Dad made do with old clothes and pulled in his belt tightly on any personal expenditures that he considered unnecessary. He set up a budget whose rules were: "This money for Nancy's golf; this money for the house; this money for my job." In that order.

The saddest thing in my life so far has been Mom's unexpected death just before I won my first professional tournament. She had an appendix operation and everything seemed to be all right and then, only minutes later, she died. I was on the tour at the time but telephoning every day, and I had been completely reassured about her only an hour before Delma called to tell me the catastrophic news. Of course I dropped out of the tour and flew home to be with Dad, but the shock and the sadness about Mom is with me every day of my life. I owed her so much, and I was just on the edge of being able to repay her to some extent for all the years she lavished on me when suddenly she was gone. When I finally did go back on the tour, I won my first professional tournament and I've always felt that the toughening experience of such a tragedy might have been a factor in strengthening my determination. In any event, I dedicated that tournament to my Mom's memory, and she's never been out of my thoughts for very long ever since. Nor will she ever be. It is some consolation that she did have the joy of seeing me emerging as a star in my rookie year as a pro, and to know that I was likely to fulfill the promise she wanted so badly for me, but I certainly wish she were still here to share in what has happened since.

Once the constant agony of missing Mom had lessened a bit with time, Dad did the expected and became both father and mother to me, as well as golf teacher. There was not enough money for professional lessons but, as things have turned out, I guess Dad was all the teacher I needed. Always a very good golfer himself and sporting a 3-handicap at the time (he still plays to a 12-handicap now in his mid-sixties), he is really the only coach I've ever had. I watched him and he showed me the basics, but apart from instructing me regularly to "come up real slow, come up real high, extend real far and hit the ball right in the sweet spot and hit it right in the middle of the fairway, and then keep hitting it until you hit it into the hole," he didn't elaborate too much. I did what he told me and it seemed to work: The ball did usually fly long and straight, so Dad left my swing alone and ever since he has only tipped me off when I seem to him to be having some trouble because I've been slipping away from my natural swing in one respect or another.

That doesn't happen so often that I've ever been tempted to do too much analyzing of my game, or let anyone else advise me. Recently I was shown a very funny golf story written years ago by the famous humorist, P. G. Wodehouse, entitled "The Heel of Achilles." It was about a dynamic man, a financier with a will of iron, who wanted to marry a woman who couldn't bear him, but also was incapable of saying "No" outright to such a man. So she set him the impossible task of winning the national championship that year to prove his worth. He had never heard of golf, let alone played it, but he had a pro come to his office and explain the basic idea in ten minutes, which was all the time he could spare since he was cornering Woven Textiles that morning.

Well, he shot scratch golf the very first time out, and he went to the final of the amateur championship without ever losing a hole. (He lost the final because of his "Achilles' heel," but you'll have to read the story yourself if you want to know what that was.) The point of my telling you about it at all here is because there's a paragraph in that story which, in an admittedly exaggerated way, seems to apply to some extent to how Dad taught me golf. Here it is:

> Golf is in its essence a simple game. You laugh in a sharp, bitter, barking manner when I say this, but nevertheless it is true. Where the average man goes wrong is in making the game difficult for himself. Observe the non-player, the man who walks round with you for the fresh air. He will hole out with a single care-free flick of his umbrella the twenty-foot putt over which you would ponder and hesitate for a full minute before sending it off the line. Put a driver into his hands and he pastes the ball into the next county without a thought. It is only when he takes the game in earnest that he becomes self-conscious and anxious, and tops his shots even as you and I. A man who could retain through his golfing career the almost scornful confidence of the non-player would be unbeatable.

*Delma is always a
faithful rooter*

Well, that story isn't about me, but farfetched as its general idea is, there is no denying that Dad kept things simple and that I responded to such teaching. He's very good at spotting any slips and I couldn't imagine anyone more supportive and noncritical, and that's what seems to be best for me. Whenever he can he leaves his business for a while and comes to see me play in a tournament. He doesn't say much, but when he does I listen carefully. Dad only went to the third grade in school, but he's as smart about people as he is about golf. He was really good-looking when he was young, as I've seen in photos, and today I think he's cuter than ever. He's on the small side but very distinguished-looking, with graying sideburns that I particularly like, and his skin is an even, wonderful, warm tan. I've always loved my family's looks. My mother was very pretty and had the silkiest skin all her life. Both Delma and I seem to have inherited that, along with the need to keep up the battle against excess poundage to some extent, but I think we've been lucky about our looks in most respects. Remember the young girl in Thornton Wilder's play *Our Town* who kept pestering her mother about whether she was pretty or not? And finally the mother lost her patience and said that she was pretty enough "for all practical purposes"? I don't think it would be immodest either for Delma or me to claim the same. And that's enough about that. This is a book about golf.

The real indication that I might indeed turn out to be the golfer my parents hoped I'd be came within a year after my first experience on Roswell's municipal course. I was entered in a PeeWee tournament being held in Alamogordo, New Mexico, for girls between the ages of eight and twelve. It was a twenty-seven-hole affair held over a three-day period and I won it by a margin of 110 strokes! Dad was so excited and pleased that as an extra prize he bought me my favorite present at that time, a Barbie doll! That set a dangerously expensive precedent for him, because I was so crazy about Barbie dolls that I never could get too many. It wasn't that I actually played with them the way I did when I was even younger, but I had begun to be a collector. You've heard of the fastest gun in the West? Well I was building up the biggest collection of Barbie dolls in the West. Each time after that when I did something special in golf, Dad came through with a doll that meant more to me than any medal or cup. By the time I was twelve I already had a great many and then, when I won the Women's State Amateur (Women's, not Girls') at that age, he came home with a whole armful! I may have reached the ripe old age of twelve, and I may have shot a course record of 75 at the University South course in Albuquerque in the run toward winning the state championship, but collecting Barbie dolls was still Big Stuff! Dad said, "Nancy win. Nancy get every doll in the shop!"

You may have noticed the way Dad speaks? We are, of course, Mexican Americans, and that brings up the second obstacle to my getting an easy early golf education to which I referred earlier in this chapter. Dad has a strong Spanish accent and flavor to his speech and, although that didn't rub off on a girl who grew up so Americanized as I did in school and with Anglo friends, all of us Lopezes are definitely and unashamedly Mexican Americans in Roswell, a town where that surely wasn't a social asset. It's a very pleasant town of some 40,000 people, and I have good memories of it, but we had the sort of minority status that minorities invariably suffer everywhere. In my case, it certainly never was any tragedy, and just about all of my friends were Anglos and good friends, but one could get snubbed when one least expected it. I remember once dating a boy and his parents hit the roof when they heard about it. Today when someone tells me that certain old "friends" from Roswell send me warm regards, I sometimes have to take it with a grain of salt. A few of those old "friends" don't raise tender memories.

The point is that while I could play on the municipal course, that wasn't a well-kept, regulation layout that could have challenged my developing game better. It was only a nine-hole layout then, not well trapped, and its chief virtue was that you could play there for something like $1.25. Roswell had several things to boast about, including being John Denver's hometown, but one of its prides was the country club with its first-rate golf course. The dues there would have been pretty tough for Dad to manage, but the whole idea was academic anyhow. Mexican Americans like my parents would not have been welcome members, and if they didn't join I obviously couldn't and wouldn't. As a matter of fact, I'm sure I wouldn't have been happy in that atmosphere in any event because, although people were perfectly nice to me when I played at the club in a city tournament, I was just as happy to get away between rounds. There was a polite frostiness about the whole place that made me quite reconciled to going back and playing on the municipal course.

Actually a short while later it turned out not to matter that I didn't have the advantage of being able to use the club course. When I became amateur state champion, the mayor of the city not only gave me free use of my old friend, the municipal course, but also free golf privileges on another infinitely better city golf course, located on a military school's grounds right there in Roswell. So I got plenty of good golf play from then on, without the frills.

I sometimes wonder what would have happened if a teaching professional from a country club had latched onto me at that stage. My Dad left my natural game alone, but I don't know if a pro could have resisted taking me apart and putting me together again, because I know that my swing is regarded as neither conventional nor stylish. But I felt comfortable with it and still do, particularly ever since the time I had a chance to query a fellow Mexican American, Lee Trevino, about it. I said, "Mr. Trevino, what should I do about my golf swing? I have a bad golf swing and yet I play very well."

Trevino didn't ask me to show him my swing at all. Instead he simply said, "You can't argue with success. If you swing badly but still score well and win, don't change a thing."

That was quite a while back but I never forgot what he

An early win—the Trans-National back in 1976

said and so far, at least, he's turned out to be right. The less I analyze my swing, the better off I believe myself to be. I will think about aspects of my game, like keeping my cool and concentrating when the chips are down, but except when putting (which is a separate game) I don't worry about the mechanics of a stroke. I do what Dad taught me: "Come up on the backswing real slow and real high, extend, and hit the ball."

Do you feel cheated? You paid your good money for a book that at least in part was supposed to tell you how I played golf, and *that's* all that I have to tell you about the full golf swing? Yes, it easily could have been if someone hadn't practically pointed a gun at my head and made me think about it. What happened was this.

The magazine, *Golf Digest*, signed me up to be a "Playing Editor," and since golf instruction is what they want for the most part, it became clear that I'd better sit down and try analyzing what makes my golf swing tick, if I was going to earn my keep. So for once I really thought hard about it and, in the end, I think it came out well. Probably that's because the sequence of photographs is super and you know what they say—a picture is worth a thousand words. In any case, here is the gist of what I wrote in the magazine article that accompanied the picture spread, as well as the photos themselves.

I know some people consider my swing unorthodox, but in analyzing the sequence of tee-shot photographs I see the application of quite a few fundamentals. The setup is fine, the tempo is smooth and the clubface is square coming through the ball. I remember hitting a particularly good shot when these photos were taken.

The key to my swing is tempo. I have a very slow tempo, which I feel reduces the margin of error. With a fast tempo, you never swing the same way twice in a row. Under pressure, the temptation is to swing even faster. I know, because I used to have a fast swing. Now that I've slowed it down, I feel far more comfortable over the ball.

I recommend a slow swing tempo particularly for women amateurs who are anxious to improve their games. If you're wondering how you generate power with a slow backswing, the reason is that power comes from clubhead speed, which is generated on the downswing. The backswing merely gets the club in position for the downswing.

How do I keep my tempo slow? Well, I concentrate on it. I try very hard, on each shot, to take the club back low and slow. I stress tempo in practice. When you practice well, you're training your muscles to swing exactly the same all the time. You could lay off for a month and come back and your muscles would swing the same because they've been trained that way. Muscle memory is the term. If you ask me how you can improve, I suggest that you find a swing that feels comfortable and works consistently. Practice that swing, and your muscles will train themselves to execute it that way time after time.

People who watch me play often remark that I don't turn my hips as much as most women on tour. I don't. I have more of what I call top action—I use the upper half of my body. When I'm swinging my arms and turning my shoulders on the backswing, I feel I'm winding up like a spring. The spring tightens and tightens until I can feel the strain in my upper body. Then all that tension releases in the downswing.

One thing everybody seems to comment about is that little hand hitch I have at address. I have a comparatively upright stance, and at address my hands are low. I feel comfortable in this position at the start. Then I lift my hands a few inches before I start the backswing. This gets

Here I am at address. I try to make sure I'm upright, not slouched like some players. My knees are flexed slightly and my stance is square. My right arm is more relaxed than the left, which is firm. My weight is distributed fairly evenly, just a little more on the right leg than the left.

Just before starting the backswing, I raise my hands a couple of inches. It's a personal technique I have that gets me set. Then I take the clubhead back low and slow. Notice that I haven't started to turn my shoulders or body yet.

With the clubhead still low to the
ground and my arms swinging freely,
I'm starting to turn my shoulders.
I've already broken my wrists. I do
this sooner than most players, because
that's the way I learned to swing. My
head has not moved.

Nearly halfway through the takeaway,
my weight is still nearly balanced,
with a little more on the right side.
The shoulders are turning and I'm
starting to feel my upper body coiling
like a spring. The left knee is
gradually sliding back toward the
right.

Notice the arms here. My left arm is firm and my right elbow is tucked. The weight is shifting more to the right side, the left side remaining firm. The top part of my body is feeling tighter and tighter. . .

. . . until I feel like a wound-up spring at the top of my backswing. The clubhead here is a little out of position and the clubface is shut, but on the downswing my hands maneuver it into the proper position. I don't raise my left heel; it's flat on the ground.

As the downswing begins, the weight starts shifting to the left side, and I'm pushing off my right leg, which is braced. The legs, which haven't had much to do so far, are starting their real work.

My backswing plane is a little flat and I tend to get the club "laid off" behind me. But here, in my downswing, the plane is more upright and my hands and the clubface are in the proper relationship. My left arm is firm, my weight continues to shift to the left and my right knee is driving toward the target.

Here we go. I'm coming down into the ball with plenty of leg action. My hands, body, shoulders and legs are all in proper position. I'm square to the target line, not open or blocked out. I like the way my right elbow is still tucked in.

Crack! I have just made contact with the ball. My wrists have uncocked with a snapping motion and my lower body has cleared to let them through. The clubhead is still low to the ground. I'm hitting against a very firm left side, which is good. My head is still down.

This is what I call good extension. My arms and the club are flying toward the target, propelled by a strong push off my right leg. The force of my swing has started to pull my head up to allow a full finish . . .

. . . which is exactly what I have here. The club has whipped all the way around over my shoulders, and my body is facing squarely at the target. My right knee is relaxed, my left knee firm. My weight is on my left side. Not a bad swing!

me set. It serves the same purpose as a forward press.

Unlike many pro golfers, I keep my left heel on the ground during the backswing: it firms up my whole left side. If I lift my heel, I feel as though I'm letting my left side collapse. If you have the flexibility, it's a good way to play, I think.

I get a lot of power by pushing off on my right leg on the downswing. I can feel the pressure on my right foot digging in, giving me the strength that I want for getting through the shot. At the same time, my left leg is firm as I shift my weight from the right side to the left side. My wrists uncock and sort of snap right through the ball. Hearing that click as the result of good hand and arm action is one of the most beautiful sounds in golf.

My follow-through is a big, sweeping extension of the swing. I just let everything go, as though I couldn't stop the swing if I wanted to. The club is wrapped around my shoulders, and my entire body is facing the target. I notice so often in watching women amateurs that they quit on the swing right after impact. How much more effective it is to sweep the club through with a full extension!

Over the years I have maintained pretty much a right-to-left ball action. It gets me a little extra distance, particularly off the tee. But more recently, I have hit a lot of perfectly straight shots, especially during the time I was winning five tournaments in a row. I had great faith in my swing. My drives were splitting the fairways and I was hitting a number of good iron shots near the flag. The better I played, the more my confidence grew. It was a wonderful feeling.

I've never claimed to have a picture-book swing, like Mickey Wright does, but I do have a comfortable and reliable swing that repeats under pressure. I feel that I hit the ball solidly and accurately enough. I built this swing through long hours of practice. I still need a lot of practice to keep it sharp, and that's why I log my share of hours on the range.

That's the general story of how I hit a golf ball, but if you really want to ponder about it in depth, the photographs and their captions convey the idea in much fuller, textbook style. But *you* do it because, now that I've completed my job, I just want to forget it all and go back to doing what now comes naturally.

Chapter 2

I Got Rhythm

My Education in Dynamics

ROSCOE JONES, my caddie, and I hit the interstate highways every Monday during the season, driving long distances from tournament to tournament. One of the things that helps make it fun is that we're always yakking with other drivers on the road over the CB network. I think CB's are great. You get and give each other tips on how to avoid the worst traffic, where to exit off a highway, what's the best place to grab a bite or to get gas. But apart from its usefulness, just jabbering away with the truckers and other drivers helps keep you awake and lively.

My CB handle is "Jive Cookie," and I guess it fits me pretty well—at least the "Jive" part of it—because I'm really hung up on disco and jazz and rock music. As for "Cookie" . . . well . . . maybe. All pop music is a big thing with me and whenever life shapes up so that I've got to pack my things and move, which has happened quite a lot over the past year or two, my stereo and tapes get first attention after my golf gear. My motto is get the clubs safely into the car, then pack the stereo stuff into the trunk very, very carefully, and finally think about what else I ought to take along in setting up a new home.

And music ties into cars somehow in my mind, and that may simply be because I'm car-nutty as well, as you'll find out, and a tape deck setup installation is about the same sort of "optional" in my mind in buying a car as is power steering. That's how "rhythm" works into the picture I'm trying to give you of myself, and if it strikes you as a little farfetched in what's supposed to be a golf book, it really isn't. I think rhythm of several sorts is kind of built into me, and one form of it is the absolute keynote of my golf game. That's tempo. I'll get to that a couple of pages further on, but first, since this is an autobiography as well as a book about golf, let me tell you about my love affair with cars and pop music. It goes back a long way, but not as long as the song "I Got Rhythm." I wasn't conscious, until I looked it up, that it was a famous Gershwin song sung forty or fifty years ago by Ethel Merman. To me it had been a swinging number sung by Barbra Streisand.

I got my first driver's license in Roswell when I was fifteen years old. You'll remember that by then I was playing regular amateur competition golf, and both my parents and I were serious about my making a possible career in the professional game. Dad asked me what my vote would be. Should the Lopezes sell their house and buy another near the golf course, or did I want him to get me a car so I could drive there myself every day instead of having my mother ferry me all the time in the family car? Well, apart from the fact that I figured the car would be much cheaper, because I was expecting a Volkswagen or something like that, there was no choice in my mind. I was tremendously excited about the idea of having my own car, and a Volkswagen would have been just great, I thought. But although I thought I knew my Dad, I didn't anticipate what he actually came up with for me. It was a brand new 1972 Gran Torino, with the big tires and the silver rims and everything, including a first-rate AM/FM radio. Kids are likely to blame their parents for everything. I've got to blame my Dad for getting me hooked onto cars. That canary yellow beauty really blew my mind. My parents probably picked out the color so they could spot me easily around town when they were looking for me. Not that anyone had to look very hard, for I loved showing the car off. It had a very distinctive horn, and I was apt to use it more than I needed to as I drove down the main drag in Roswell. And although I never did drive fast, and still don't, I did like to take off from a stand-still pretty quickly and make that screeching noise with the tires—burning rubber. That got me the nickname of "Skeetch" when I took the car away to college. That's just about my only nickname unless you count CB's "Jive Cookie" as one, and on the tour in my rookie year some of the women called me "Kid." A few good friends, like Roscoe, occasionally called me "Lopes."

After a while, Dad figured the skeetching Gran Torino was getting kind of too young-looking for me, and kind of too old-looking for itself, and he wanted me to have a good new reliable car to travel in when I went on the tour. So he bought me a maroon Monte Carlo with an eight-track tape deck and an FM stereo radio in it. He said: "Well, Nancy, this is the last car I'm buying. The next one you're going to have to buy for yourself." That sure was fair enough, but with the first money I made on the tour.I simply improved the Monte Carlo. I bought a CB for it.

Since then I haven't had to buy a car because whenever I especially need one, the Frontier Ford Agency in Albuquerque lets me have a brand new Thunderbird, or something of the sort, to use. It's part of a contract I have to do a few commercials for them, and they fix me up with a new car every 8,000 or 9,000 miles, but of course I don't really own those cars. So when Tim and I decided to get married, we wanted a van of our own that we could travel together in, and we bought a customized Ford van that's real neat.

We went half-and-half on the cost of it, which makes us both feel it's ours and not just something borrowed. Of course, if any of us golfers ever makes a hole-in-one at the right time at the right place on the right hole, a car company is likely to give the lucky performer a car, but that's never happened to me. Tim and I didn't figure it was worth waiting around for, since the odds against it must be something like a million to one. You can't exactly plan on getting a car that way.

The fact is that I've made four holes-in-one in my life, and all four were in the same year, when I was fifteen! Two of them came in the same month, then another the next month, then I missed a month, but I shot the last one the month after that. It was really weird. Right before the first one I asked my Dad when he thought I'd ever make a hole-in-one and he said Arnold Palmer had never made one, and he was not only the best but had been playing a long time. So I thought, well—maybe I'll never make one either, but then I shot four in a row! Three of them were on standard, fairly short par-3 holes, but one was about a 220-yard-long par-3, which I went at with a 4-wood. I was playing in a crowd with six boys, because the course was kind of empty since it was pouring down rain. My shot went right at the pin, hit it, and the ball plunked down into the hole! A couple of the guys said they saw and heard the splash it made, and they all signed my scorecard. I still have it tucked away somewhere.

The time I came closest to winning a car with a hole-in-one was when I was winning my first pro tournament at Bent Tree. I hit a 6-iron on a short hole and the ball actually went into the cup but then popped out again, an inch or so away. And that would have won me a Cadillac! Roscoe was so mad! He said he *thought* he had given me the right club for the shot!

That's almost enough about cars, except I have to tell you one more thing before I get back to golf. In the middle of my rookie year, when I was doing so well and being interviewed a lot, a reporter asked me what I wanted next. I answered: "A Mercedes 450 SL, just like any other red-blooded American girl would." And now I'm driving one! The Mercedes people let me have the use of a beautiful red one *with a tape deck* and I really love it. Trouble is, it's not mine, and the idea is that I'll give it back after a while, but I've started to think about that. I'm not sure I could bear to say good-bye.

Rhythm, Pace, Tempo. They're all connected to each other and they're all a part of me. But while I like the lively and the fast and bouncy in one part of my life, in golf I've learned to use my inborn feelings for those attributes in a different way. On the golf course I think about my tempo every time I swing a club, but the tempo is slow and even and controlled. It's the foundation of my game, right from the drive along to the putt.

I can't pin down exactly where and when my simple technique was drilled into me. That very slow backswing with a very full extension, all performed with the same tempo on every shot that includes a pause at the top and a continued full extension on the downswing, just seemed natural from the start. I guess at first it was a copy of my father's swing, and even though my swing has been criticized as being unorthodox, it works. I've made some very minor adjustments over the years but no real change at all. I told you about my swing in the last chapter, but I never want to think too much about how I hit a golf ball when I'm actually out there hitting one because, if I do, I'm afraid I won't hit it as well as I seem to do instinctively.

But I can tell you what I concentrate upon when playing,

Right from the drive . . .

. . . along to the putt

and maybe you'll find it interesting and even helpful. It's not going to be much of the stuff you read in golf instruction books about grips, and stances, and pronation, and unleashing of the cock of the wrists, and all that. That makes me dizzy. I think golf instruction is likely to give you more complicated words and actions to think about than you can possibly swallow, and certainly more than you can digest all at the same time while you're trying to hit a golf ball. My prescription is simple, and it's the same one Dad gave me when I was eight years old. Hit the ball and keep hitting it until you find your natural swing. Then practice, practice, practice, until it's so grooved that you can do it in your sleep.

Saying "find your natural swing" goes against the idea that there's an absolutely right way and a lot of wrong ways to play golf. It seems to me that there is no sure and fixed "right way." Perhaps there is a best way for most people, but there are enough glaring examples of unorthodox players who are fine, and even great ones, for me to question whether any aspect of usual golf teaching is sacred. As an example, take Arnold Palmer. Take Judy Rankin. Take me. None of us would be a model for a film of a classic golf swing. There have been great golf players who used a baseball grip, players who prefer to fade an approach onto a green and those who prefer to draw one into it, players who always pitch right to the hole and try to hold the ball there and others who, under certain conditions, much prefer to pitch and run the shot. There may well be a best way for most people but there's no best way for everybody.

It makes sense to me, therefore, *not* to be overtutored at the very beginning. Maybe it's just because I wasn't and it all worked out fine for me. Admittedly, that's awfully personal and maybe self-centered, but I just wonder if it isn't better not to approach golf in such a complicated way. How about just getting out and banging away for quite a while at first, exactly as any kid would do in any other game on a country lot or a city street? A person with any aptitude at all for hitting a ball with an implement will manage to do so without being told too much, and he or she will get better at it with more and more practice. After a while, very probably some expert advice may help to polish the rough spots, but I really think that finding your own tempo and groove at first is the best recipe. Mentally as well as physically, because it makes the approach to the sport fun instead of hard work, like going to school.

Of course, as in all sustained efforts, you've got to be intrigued about what you're trying to do, and care enough to keep at it. Golf seems such a super game to me that I'd think it likely to be appealing to almost anyone, but I remember what interested and impressed me most when I started following Dad and Mom. It was the sound of their golf shoes when they walked on a hard surface like cement. I loved the sound the cleats made, and at the beginning I wanted golf shoes for myself just to walk around in much more than I wanted golf clubs to play with!

But by the time I inherited Mom's bag of clubs, I wanted to play all right, and Dad pounded it into me that practice was the answer, once he saw I could connect with a ball. He showed me the right way to practice too. You can't just go out and whack balls. Lots of people do that without ever thinking about what they're doing. You have to learn something about yourself and your strokes when you practice, or it's a waste of time. It may be helpful in certain of those things I'm emphasizing, like establishing your tempo and grooving your swing, just to hit ball after ball, but that alone is not enough to be called a really good practice session. Not if you're serious about your game. You have to practice your weaknesses. Even if you're actually capable of pulling

*You've got to practice
your weaknesses
regularly*

off any shot on occasion, you have to practice the most on those you don't pull off regularly enough to be sure you have the control to do so when you need it.

I like to warm up for a little while, just hitting out a few balls easily to loosen up, and then play something like nine holes. If in the course of that I find I'm not hitting my 5-irons well, for example, or pulling my 3-woods, I'll stop actual play and tail off to the practice area. There I'll work on those trouble spots until I feel I have them better in hand. I always put all my emphasis on hitting straight, because I have confidence in my basic swing at any distance. So distance is rarely the problem. And I don't often practice hitting various trick shots that admittedly you have to use now and then, like a low fade or hook to get around and under a tree. You must learn to hit such shots, and you do if you play a lot, but they don't come up so often that I think you should spend time on the practice range working on them. I'd rather work and work to straighten out the shots that I seem to have been hitting off line. If I succeed in doing so, I'm not going to get into much trouble. I like to see the shot I'm trying to make first in my mind's eye, and also actually sort of feel it with my arms and hands and body. You can do that, and I'm sure it absolutely helps you hit the ball well when you really get down to doing it. That works well for me on everything from a drive, through the occasional tricky trouble shot and the blast out of a bunker, to the putt.

Practicing putting religiously is maybe the most important of all. Even if I've been putting like a fiend over the nine holes I've played, I always finish off a practice session by going to the practice green. You can't get too much of it, because most of the time all of the top golfers are likely to reach the green in the number of strokes they should. Getting the ball into the hole after that is what wins, and

That one's a birdie!

Oops!
That one's a bogey.

that's why constant putting practice is a must. Half the strokes that constitute par on a golf course are figured to be putts, and if you can average less than the expected two putts per green, that's the way to shave par and sometimes murder it. After I won those five tournaments in a row, and then seemed to slump off for a short time, I was actually playing just as well as ever right up to the green. I was hitting the ball fine, but I wasn't getting the putts into the hole the way I usually can. That made the entire difference at the time, and when I got my putting touch back again on the trips to England and the Far East, I became a winner again.

I don't want to play rounds on a course too many times right before a tournament. Lots of golfers do, thinking that the more familiar they are with the layout, the better advantage they'll have. Maybe so, but I think you're liable to wear yourself out and leave your best game out there on the course before the event ever starts. So I want primarily to get all the distances down pat on my card, because that's the thing that I really need to know, and then just play the course once to get the feel of the terrain. After that I simply work on the practice stuff, and particularly on putting to get the texture and speed of the greens in my mind. If I do more I can get tired, both in my swing and mentally, and the mental part of competitive golf is an overwhelmingly big part. At least it is for me.

Back in the beginning, when I was using my mother's clubs, I didn't want them cut down for me. I tried having one club cut down and it was just too short then, so I left the others alone. Mom's clubs were regular-length Patty Bergs, and I was a tall, skinny kid with long arms who could handle them okay. (Yes, I was *skinny!* I ran in three events on the Mesa School track team back then.) But although I had and still have big feet, my hands were small, and I think that's why the interlocking grip felt better to me than the more usual overlapping grip. So I started out interlocking, and I still do.

There's one thing that I imagine I did instinctively, or maybe I copied Dad. Although I had adult clubs that might have been a shade too long for my size, I didn't stand far away from the ball when addressing it, and that could have been a natural result under the circumstances. In other words, I didn't develop a flat swing, which many beginners do, and that's why the most chronic trouble that beginners have is a slice. They swing from the outside and cut across the ball. Maybe they've played other games, like baseball or tennis, where the swing is horizontal and it's good to keep the ball as far away from your hands as possible. So a flat golf swing makes them feel they can get more power into the stroke. But it's not right for golf. The golf stroke is essentially a vertical one, and you ought to be quite upright in your stance in addressing the ball. I don't know who originated the phrase, but I've heard one old, very vivid piece of instruction about this, which was given to a person whose swing was too flat. It was: "Get off the merry-go-round and get onto the Ferris wheel!"

Once I had gotten pretty good at golf, I'd occasionally see things in other players' strokes that impressed me, and then I'd try to work them into my own game without making any fundamental changes. I never want to tamper in any way with things like my rhythm and tempo, but quite early in my amateur career I was lucky enough to see Carol Mann and Kathy Whitworth play, and I saw that each of them anchored her left foot on the ground and didn't allow the heel to come up. I hadn't been doing that, but I liked the way it looked and it struck me as logical. If I kept my left foot firmly down, it would make my backswing tighter and make my body turn into more of a spring, coiled to come down into the ball a lot better. It made common sense to me, so I tried it and it worked, and that's been a part of my technique ever since. It's one other contribution I picked up from watching star players, like my having to give Donna Caponi Young credit for my very slow backswing. I had never been prone to rush a shot, but watching Donna do so well with a backswing even slower made me realize how foolish it is ever to take the club back fast. The ball isn't going to run away, and you don't have to hurry things as if you had to chase it.

The slowness with which I take the club back now develops into a slight pause that I make at the top, before starting down. It's all part of the tempo I try to establish and keep doing shot after shot—the rhythm. I don't count numbers, or whistle a happy tune or anything, but constant practice has established that rhythm so that I now can count on it.

Though I've never really had formal golf instruction other than Dad's, I've picked up small things here and there like the ones I latched onto after watching Carol and Kathy. At Tulsa University, the team pro was Buddy Phillips and while he left my game alone essentially, he did change my grip a little. I had my right hand a bit too far under the club, so that the palm faced up toward the sky, and I'd been letting the club rest in the palm. Buddy had me take the club more into my fingers and turn my hand a bit counterclockwise so that the palm faced the target. It helped a lot. I had been slicing, and with just this little change I started to draw the ball instead, and I liked that infinitely more. The impact felt much more solid, and the ball got a considerably longer roll after landing.

Dale McNamara was our coach and she was a strong supporter of mine, for which I'll always be grateful to her, but she really didn't work on my technique at all. Her job was more administrative. There was a good friend of mine named Rick Gutierrez, who was a golf pro at Albuquerque, and one day after watching me he offered what turned out to be a valuable piece of advice about chipping. I thought I had always been a good chipper, you know, from just off the fringe of the green, but Rick said he thought I could be better. He suggested I open my stance just a bit and move my hands forward, like a forward press, when I addressed the ball, and he said not to break my wrists but keep them firm all the way through the shot. That did make my chipping even better, and I tip my eyeshade to Rick, but that about ends it as far as the faculty in my education as a golfer is concerned.

I've taken those things I've seen, and those suggestions that have been given to me, and if they made sense and worked, I've incorporated them into my practice until I've got them down pat. Then they've become as much a part of my tempo and coordination as all the other things. Co-ordination is almost everything, and the other big factor for me is confidence. If you have both, you've got it. I remember once looking at a shot and thinking, "I wonder how I ever hit this small ball with this little bitty clubface," and I swear I almost whiffed! I made the mistake of *thinking* about the difficulty of a shot, and that's a mistake I haven't allowed myself to make since. The only things I think about when playing are the ones I've written about, and picking out the right club to do the job, because I hit all my long shots virtually the same way. Same preparation, same extended arc, same length of backswing, altogether the same overall pattern. Of course there are small variations in the way I play a wood from the way I play an iron, which I'll go into in the next paragraph, and I play the long irons more off my left heel than I do the shorter ones. As the numbers on the irons increase, I address the ball farther back toward the center of my stance, and by the time I'm using a pitching iron the ball is not too much to the left of my right foot. But the swing and the tempo are the same for all of them. If I ever have to make a shot where I don't seem to have a club that's exactly right for the distance (remember you can only carry fourteen clubs and that means you can't have every single type of club made), I'll select the club that may be a shade too strong for the distance and choke down a little on the grip, making the length of the shaft that much shorter. That will cut the distance I'd get using the full length by just about the right amount, and it means I can take my regular full swing and not have to spare the shot. I don't purposely open the clubface or close it either, as some people do under special circumstances. For me a square face is the best way to play all shots.

On fairway woods, I keep the same swing but I don't hit *down* on the ball the way I do with irons. Irons require that you hit down into the shot, connecting with the ball first and then keep going down through it so that your clubhead punches into the turf and takes a divot. With woods on the fairway I hit down very little, but just kind of pick the ball off the grass while the clubhead makes a furrow on the ground, but it's nothing like the divot an iron shot makes. You sort of shave the grass with the woods, like shaving your face. You don't draw blood.

With the driver, which has the ball teed up so nicely, you don't hit down at all, but you sweep the ball off the tee with your full swing, and maybe you're even hitting up on it a little at actual impact, because of the fact that it's sitting up there above the ground.

I go just as far back on my swing with every shot, whether it's a wood or an iron, a long shot or a comparatively short one. I aim to have my swing so absolutely consistent that I never have to think about that. That's the only way I feel sure of what I'm doing, and being sure instills confidence.

My intention is to go back just far enough that at the top of the backswing the shaft of the club will be parallel to the ground, and that's what I do when I'm swinging my best, but I do have a tendency to overswing a bit. But if I extend and keep my tempo, coordination will compensate and bring me back into the right position to come into the shot. That's why I try never to vary my swing no matter what the shot situation may be, because if my swing is solid I won't hit the ball flat, or hit the ground behind it. I *know* that my club will come through into where the ball is sitting patiently waiting for it, if I just do my thing and keep doing it. As long as I didn't think about it (which I'm afraid I might if I tried it), I believe I could hit a golf ball well with my eyes shut.

Sometimes people wonder why so much emphasis is put upon the follow-through in golf instruction. I remember being upset once and telling my Dad I wasn't following through right, and he replied, "Nancy, it doesn't make any difference to a ball what you do after you hit it." Of course, that seems to make sense, but I think I do know why you must follow through correctly. If you don't, you haven't extended to the utmost on your downswing, and if you don't do that, you haven't done the job. But if you do extend properly all the way to meet the ball at impact, the extension simply automatically makes you keep going with your swing out toward the target. So the follow-through is the effect that comes from the cause, because you can't hit a ball right and just stop and collapse. If you do, you didn't hit the ball right. The follow-through may therefore only be the clue to what you have done, but if you make a good follow-through part of the groove you develop through constant practice of your swing, it stands to reason that in getting to it you'll have done the right thing along the way, when it counted.

Here's the thing of it about extending. As I take my club back, I try to keep the clubhead as low to the ground as possible for as long as I can. That gets the extension going. Then I try to retain it all the way back to the top of the swing, keeping my left arm straight with no bend to maintain the full arc, and that holds true on the downswing too. The idea is to come down far out and back low along the ground as you get near the ball, just the way you went up but in reverse. I don't think at all about other stuff that's in traditional golfing dogma, like coming into the ball from the inside out, because that sort of thing just happens naturally if you extend and hit through smoothly, and all the way. Your body and your coordination do the job if you've got the basic idea, and have practiced enough to fit things into your groove. Whenever I happen to overhear a golf lesson or clinic, it usually seems mechanical to me and the sort of thing that's likely to mess me up. I don't really want to know that my arm's not set right, or the cock of my wrist is wrong. I can feel it when something's not going the way it should feel, so I just plug away at practice until it comes around and does feel right again.

Take the pressure I apply with my hands on the grip. Without really thinking about it, I'm conscious of the fact that I grip considerably tighter with my left hand, both going up and most of the way down, because the left hand is the real control. The power of the right hand isn't brought into play until just before the impact with the ball. But I don't ever *think* about that—things like "unleashing the power in the right hand." If I'm not hitting the ball as well as I should it just *feels* wrong, and it's going to feel right again if I go out and practice some more. Maybe I was doing this or that wrong, and maybe the correction I made was indeed something that a golf pro might have spotted and told me about before I was able to feel good about things myself. But I've been successful working matters out my own way, and I know that if I think about all the things you're supposed to analyze, I'll be in trouble.

You want to feel relaxed whenever you play golf, and it starts when you position yourself as you address the ball. If you're tense and stiff, you can't get any kind of motion going with your legs, and that's bad because you do use your legs a lot in a golf swing. I stand up easy with my legs relaxed. As I take the club back, I keep a firm right side and as my body turns, my right knee straightens. My left foot stays firmly planted right on the ground, as I told you earlier. Now I begin to feel that I'm winding up into a tight spring position, and my shoulders, arms, and my whole back are tightening the spring while that left foot anchors it. I don't worry about turning my hips at all, as I understand is taught by some instructors, because if I turn my shoulders properly everything else has to turn with them. That's it on the backswing as far as I'm concerned, and it may be too uncomplicated or even not right for everybody to learn from it, but it points up my chief philosophy. Try to hit the ball in your natural way, perhaps modifying in small particulars later, but at the beginning don't get fouled up by trying to learn a million mechanical details that feel unnatural to you.

Finally, let's move on to that part of golf where you really have a big chance to make your score respectable, even if you're not the best golfer in the world, and where the champions get their edge over the merely very good ones —putting. Anytime somebody is on a hot putting streak in a tournament, you've probably got the winner. There's no point in putting your approach shot eight feet from the hole while your opponent puts hers twenty feet from it, if she then sinks her putt and you miss yours.

Putting skill develops from practice, practice, practice. Plus supreme confidence after a while. The practice part of it is obvious, because every course and even different greens on the same course have varying textures and rolls and speeds. You can only learn how to judge them and handle them from experience, and you don't get enough experience just playing. You must practice lots as well. Confidence, the other factor, is a big thing all the way, and not just in putting. There was a boy on our high school team one year, a team on which I played with the boys, and he would often look at a hole from the tee and say, "Oh gosh, I'm going to bogey this one." And he almost always would when he said it, even though there was no reason for it and he was a really good stroker of the ball. You just can't think that way. It's sure to do you in, and the

A story that doesn't need words

place where lack of confidence shows up with catastrophic results most often is on the greens.

It starts sometimes when you're not quite on the green, just on the fringe or apron. If you start getting nervous because there are a few feet of grass in front of the ball before the smoother surface of the green begins, and you decide not to use your putter even though you much prefer it for a stroke of the distance that lies before you, you're on your way to blowing the shot. Sure, if the grass on the apron really presents undue difficulties, the decision to rely on an 8-iron pitch-and-run, or a pitching wedge where you try to plunk the ball close to the hole and make it hold for a short run, may be the right decision. In such a situation, I prefer the 8-iron pitch-and-run shot, because it's closer to the regular putt, and I have more confidence I can do it better. But usually the grass is not so long on the fringe as to require anything more than to take it into account, and putt with a bit more strength. So I like to use a putter for such approaches to the pin, even when the pin is a long way off. I have a lot of confidence in what I can do with the club, knowing that it's going to go straight toward what I'm aiming at, and that all I need concern myself with is the distance, and perhaps a break in the green. If the break is too severe, I may decide to rely upon a pitch, but if it's moderate I'd rather judge it, and putt.

On a really long putt, such as that is likely to be, I visualize a circle with a radius of five feet around the hole, because if I can put my ball into it, I really feel I can make any five-footer ninety-nine times out of a hundred. That's the sort of putt I practice on the most. It seems that so many tournaments are lost by missed five-footers, and won by the person who canned them all without flinching. So I visualize that circle, which really covers a pretty big area since its diameter is ten feet, and I try to make sure that my long approach putt finishes up somewhere within it, so that I'll be left with my practically sure five-footer or less. Of course, I'm also really going for the hole itself, and hoping Lady Luck will show up, but the main idea is to make sure I don't three-putt under such circumstances.

I use the interlocking grip for putting too, but fairly recently I've modified my usual grip when I putt. It's still the old interlock, but I place the index finger of my right hand down along the grip. It seems to give me a bit better control, and it keeps the putter in line better for hitting the ball squarely. A putt feels more like a brush to me than a stroke or a tap, but on slow greens I do tend to jab putts a bit because you've got to get a kind of punch into it when the greens are wet, or unnaturally slow for any other reason. When that happens you have to watch out not to get the ball bouncing, because what you always want is a roll, so even if you punch a bit more than usual, you must keep it smooth. Of course on the opposite, a lightning-fast green that's baked out, obviously you can never punch the ball. What I do then is to line the ball up with the toe of my putter rather than the "sweet spot" at the center, and give it a fairly normal stroke. The toe is the weak part of the clubface, so hitting the ball with the same strength will cut down on the roll, but you have to be careful to line the ball up squarely with the toe.

There was a time, when I first was playing, when I'd cut across a putt on purpose, and I putted well that way. I always could putt. It's a matter of feeling the ball into the hole as much as anything else, and if you see the way it's going to drop in before you ever hit it, any number of putting styles can work. But after a while I decided that cutting my putts, in other words slicing the stroke from outside the line across the ball and in, didn't really make much sense. It could go sour on me some day, and it wasn't at all consistent with my aim on every other shot, to meet the ball squarely. So I quit cutting putts and never have gone back to it since.

As far as breaks in the green are concerned, you've just got to learn from experience and practice. Slope of the terrain sometimes comes into it, even if you don't see an obvious break on the green itself. If you're near mountains or water, for example, the general thing to remember is that the green is likely to slope away from the mountains, and down toward the water. Your eyes can deceive you about this sort of thing, and using what is called the plumb-bob technique can help. That's a little hard to explain without your doing it yourself, but I'll try. Standing well behind your ball you let your putter dangle down perpendicularly from your uplifted hand, and try to line up the

Plumb-bobbing in the rain

shaft with the ball and the hole. If there's a slant in the terrain, the putter will look as if it's slanting one way or the other, instead of looking perpendicular to the ground. That's just one of the things you're apt to look over before putting. You look at the grass, how it's cut on the green that day and how dry or wet it is. Looking from some feet behind your ball at the hole, you search to see undulations and breaks that will influence the ball, and sometimes there'll be a double break. The perspective from a ways behind the hole, looking back past it at your ball, often gives you an additional and sometimes a different view about how to tackle the putt, so you walk around to there and make your inspection. Then back to your ball where by this time you should have come to the conclusion about what your line should be, so pick a spot fairly close to your ball along that line, over which you intend to start the putt off. Step up and go through whatever particular mannerisms you're accustomed to take before every putt—we all use them to settle ourselves, and it's a good idea—and then putt without agonizing over it any more, or changing your mind. It's highly doubtful that a second time around doing the same thing will be as good as your first impressions, and the very fact that you felt yourself obliged to do it bespeaks a loss of confidence, which is fatal. I suspect that's really what a famous old-time tournament professional named Macdonald Smith had in mind when he advised golfers about putting, "Miss 'em quick!" I can't believe that he meant not to examine everything carefully before actually lining up a putt, but once you've done that I agree. Except I'd make it, "Sink 'em quick!"

Putting is really life and death stuff in a big tournament, and confidence is a vital ingredient for success. There are quite a few women golfers on the tour who can hit a long ball just about as well as any of us but they don't perform overall nearly as well, and a large part of their failure comes on the greens. Elsewhere, of course, too, but where it shows up time and again is when the ball gets close to the hole. They don't get those putts down the way the top twenty or twenty-five players do, and it's not because they're incapable of it. It's more because their nerves are shaky about whether they will or not. You have to know how to scramble too, and a good scrambler most often makes up for a mistake or misfortune by canning a putt he

An engagement has been announced

or she isn't expected to make. When that happens, it makes you feel really great and it keeps you feeling that way as you tee off for the next hole, so it has a double effect. Whereas, if you're on the green in regulation figures and then three-putt, the stroke is gone forever with no chance to make it up on that hole. You're likely to want to dig an even deeper hole and crawl into it.

I know a lot of the girls feel absolutely miserable when they've played badly. It's like the end of the world. I'm no songbird myself when it happens to me, but I do know golf is only a game, and there's always another day coming up, so if I do have a disappointing day on the course, I don't feel destroyed. If you're hot on the circuit you get so many pressures anyway, and not just in playing golf, so you'd better keep your cool when you can. I got to the point once during my rookie year when I said I wasn't going to do absolutely everything people were asking me to do any longer. It was impossible—there weren't enough hours in the day. I said I was just twenty-one years old and if I had to keep going at the rate I was, I wouldn't make it to twenty-two!

Well, the fact is that I did make it on January 6, 1979. My twenty-second birthday. But by then it didn't seem too important because I had better things to celebrate on that day than my birthday. Tim and I got married and flew off to Hawaii on our honeymoon!

Chapter 3
Male and Female Created He Them

My Education in Biology

YES, THE BIBLE SAYS that He did create them, but He created them somewhat differently. You may have noticed that fact.

As far as golf is concerned, the big difference is that men have a substantial physical edge in power, so they can hit a ball a lot farther than women can. People who understand golf all that well think that golf course constructors have evened things out by establishing women's tees something like 15 to 50 yards in front of the men's tees, depending upon the length of the hole. They figure that if it's unfairly demanding to ask a woman to get home with her first shot on a 225-yard par-3 hole, cut her shot down to 210-yards and it becomes reasonable. Well, that particular case makes some sense. But they also figure that if a woman drives, let's say, an average of 225 yards, while a comparable man is driving 275 yards, then giving her a 50-yard advantage off the tee will balance matters the same way. Not true.

They forget a very big thing. Most holes are par-4's and par-5's of varying length, and even if a man's and a woman's balls are practically nestling side by side on the fairway after their drives, there's the next shot or shots coming up. If it's a par-4 hole, a man is likely to be able to use a more lofted club, something like two clubs shorter than the woman is going to need. In other words, if Jack Nicklaus and I are both 175 yards short of the flag, I'd maybe go for it with my number 4 but he wouldn't need anything more than his number 6, and anyone is going to put a lot more number 6 approaches close to the hole than they are number 4's. Whereas if a hole is a par-5, it has to be a pretty short par-5 for women to have even a chance of reaching the green in two shots and having a try for a birdie, but Tom Watson will be going for it every time, and succeeding a majority of the time.

There really is no easy answer to this problem of balancing men's and women's golf, so that their scores are likely to be level, other than placing women's tees even farther up ahead of the men's. But that would not only seem actually insulting, but also wouldn't make real sense, because then the architectural features of a golf course, designed for men's play, wouldn't work out right for a woman who might be playing very well. If a woman starts out from a tee as much as 100 yards in front of the men's tee, for example, her good drive may very well be caught by a hazard that was conceived purely to present a problem for an ordinary male golfer's second shot. So giving women even more of a distance advantage off the tee might solve some things but probably would raise even more unfair situations.

The only real answer would be for golf architects to design specific courses for women that would offer the same comparative challenges and penalties that exist on men's regulation courses, and then play the major women's tournaments on them. When I say it would be a real answer, I guess I mean a theoretical one, because economically I can't see it being very practical. Building a golf course is a very expensive proposition, and to tailor a course, or several courses, just so that tournament women golfers get the ideal is probably out of proportion to what communities would expect and want from great, costly courses the rest of the year. So what is done today, in merely having women's tees in front of the men's, is perhaps all that can be done reasonably, and it does serve its purpose fairly adequately. The only reason I've gone into what's probably an academic discussion is because the situation bugs a lot of women golfers who are aware that our seventy-two-hole totals invariably are a few strokes higher than what the men score, and people don't appreciate the real reason. They think that the tee differential ought to be enough to compensate and that we must be really poorer golfers. The fact is that a good woman golfer doesn't play the game she's physically capable of playing any less well than a man. When you take our differences in strength into consideration, and realize the problem I've explained, you'll acknowledge that we women score darned well.

I wish there were a couple of more tournaments on the tour like the Rolex International Mixed Doubles Championship, because the rules give both the men and the women a decent chance to display their skills on a fair and equal basis. The big such event in the United States is the J.C. Penney Mixed Teams Championship, held each December in Florida. Its format is a little different from the Rolex Mixed, but both draw big, enthusiastic crowds because they're both novelties and very enjoyable social events. This is how they work.

The simpler and usual rules are for the man and the woman each to drive, he from the men's tee and she from the women's. In theory, those two drives should finish pretty close to each other but then, depending upon whether that's so or not, and upon the length of the hole, the team chooses one ball or the other to play out the hole. They then alternate shots. So let's say it's a 420-yard hole and both drives are in the fairway 180 yards out from the pin. Since that sort of approach is apt to be easier for the male player, who can use a shorter club, the team is likely to select the ball the woman drove and have the man take the second shot. If he makes the green, the woman will be counted upon to make a good approach putt, or go for the possible birdie if the putt is makable.

On a par-3, where both partners reach and hold the green, they obviously select the ball closest to the hole to keep in play and let the other partner, be it the man or the woman, go for the putt. But on a long par-5, where no two shots are going to get home, the usual best strategy is to select the man's drive, have the woman hit the middle shot up the fairway as far as she can, and have the man make the approach or pitch to the green, once again leaving the first putt up to the woman. On a short par-5, where the man can reach the green with a second shot played off the woman's drive, we do select that option, just as we'd do on a par-4. That's the usual strategy, so a tournament like this involves lots of interesting choices before it's over.

I think that's the best and simplest way to play mixed doubles, and that any casual weekend foursome, consisting of two couples who like to play against each other, can have real fun playing a match of that type. A variation is to have each player hit a second shot on a hole, playing his or her partner's first ball, of course, and *then* deciding which ball to play out with alternate shots.

The most imaginative and challenging setup for this sort of event is the Rolex International Mixed Doubles Championship, held near the end of each year in Japan. Ernesto Acosta, of Mexico, and I won it in 1978, as I'll tell you later when we reach that stage of my rookie year. It's a uniquely complicated affair, designed to exhibit to the crowds a lot of different sorts of golf competition. What we did was to play two days, doing thirty-six holes on the first day. On the initial eighteen holes we alternated shots after our drives or our second shots, as described above. I really am not sure which method was used in that particular tournament: It's awfully easy to get one mixed up with another. But in any case, that first round was the alternating shots competition. Then, over the second eighteen holes. we played best ball. In other words, Ernesto Acosta and I played a regular full round independently, but we only marked down on our scorecards the better of our two scores on that hole. (In that round my 68 score won me the women's individual honors, incidentally.) In the third and last session we played total score, adding our separate tallies together each time we holed out. So it was a kind of tough three rounds, and we both had to keep really on our toes all the way not to let each other down.

That happened to be a big tournament in which I was concentrating upon bearing down and doing well but even so, with the mixture of men and all, it was a relief from the regular grind of the tour. Pro-amateur events are nice for the same reason, but I feel differently about them. Because they're not a bit important in the sense of your record for the year, I just want to relax in them and enjoy myself, but there are always big galleries around and while I like galleries, I have to admit that their presence means I can't really relax and enjoy myself completely. All I want to do in a pro-am is to have fun and hit the ball solidly, but having a gallery that has come out, expecting to see me score well, makes me keep trying to do so. That's work, not fun, and that's why I'm not crazy about pro-ams, pleasant as many of them have been.

It may be impractical for women to have golf courses designed for them, but they definitely need—and finally are getting—golf clubs designed for them. Once again, it's simply a matter of physical strength. A woman needs a lighter club if she isn't going to be dragging her tail toward the end of a long tournament, or even along the way. Without going into the really technical elaborations of golf club manufacture and specifications these days, there are whippy or flexible shafts, regular or in-between ones, and stiff and even extra-stiff ones. Unless your swing and personal preference (for whatever reason, sensible or not!) decide you to select a very whippy or a very stiff shaft, most of us go to regular shafts in the end, maybe after considerable experimentation. The theory is that a flexible shaft generates more clubhead speed on the way down and helps you get more distance, while a stiff shaft helps you be more consistently accurate in how you meet the ball. The best compromise seems to me to lie in between, so that's why I choose regulars. The other construction element in golf club manufacture is the swing weight, or the relationship of the weight at the grip end to the weight of the clubhead. Swing weights are designated with a letter and a number: A C is lighter than a D, and a 1 is lighter than a 2, and the length of the club comes into it somehow too. I don't really know all the little complexities of how and why these terms are used, but just out of experimentation and experience I find I like a swing weight of D-1, which is a long club but not too heavy. I've heard that Jack Nicklaus once used a real bludgeon, a D-6, but found it so heavy that he went all the way back to a D-1, but in the end in recent years he's settled on something in between, like a D-2 or -3 or -4, depending upon which length club it is. He's a lot more scientific about clubs than I am, and I go for a D-1 all the way. Like they say, "Different strokes for different folks!"

Many golfers today are crazy about the new graphite shafts, for instance. Janie Blalock, for one, swears by them. As for me, I'm content with steel.

I use golf clubs manufactured by Ram, and so do a great many of the women golfers. Ram clubs are allied to the Colgate people, the prime sponsors of women's golf, for one thing. The main reason I prefer them is that they're extremely good clubs.

I wear a glove on my left hand for all shots except putts. (I am, of course, right-handed.) A glove gives me a feeling of greater security in not having my grip slip on full shots. Once I reach the green I tuck my glove into the top of the back of my skirt and putt bare-handed. That's how I have the maximum "feel," which is so all-important for good putting.

I think it's both thrilling and wonderful to be female, both in being a woman and in being a woman golfer. I've never for one second regretted not being born a boy. I think Dad was rooting for me to be one because he and Mom already had one girl, my older sister, Delma. But later, although he did take me golfing and sometimes hunting, he saw to it that I was always into all the girl things, like the Girl Scouts, dolls, dresses, and all. And Mom would take me shopping with her all the time and teach me the household things right down the line. If I didn't make up my bed right she'd often actually undo it and have me make it up again properly. Maybe she'd have made a good army sergeant!

Yes, I was brought up the way a traditional girl always used to be brought up by solicitous parents and I liked it. Once I did ask Dad if he really wished I had been a boy because, for a while, he called me "Richard," the name my parents had picked out if I had turned out to be a boy. He said he was just teasing, but I suspect he might have been a little disapointed right at first, but he never really showed it once I was grown a little and I *know* he hasn't had any regrets for a long, long time. Long before I made a name in golf. My Dad wouldn't want me to be one bit different than what I am, and I feel the same way about him.

Both my parents were terribly loving and caring about me as a girl. If I had a date I had to be in like before 10:30, for instance, *always*. I sort of hated how overprotective of me they seemed to be, but now I realize that it was just because they cared so much. Back then I was always stomping my feet about it but now that I'm older I can look back and appreciate it all. Admittedly, in this era of women's lib and all that, I was brought up very old-fashioned and I guess it stuck. I still think their ways were good ways, and in a Mexican family perhaps it was even more old-fashioned than most. The man usually wants to cut a macho figure to some extent and the woman is quite happy to undertake the basic role of caring for him and the house. Today there is a more equal sharing of things, and I'm all for that, but I still value traditional roles and when the time comes when my competitive golfing days are over, and Tim and I can really settle down, I can't think of what I'd want to do with the rest of my life better than living with him in a sort of old-fashioned feminine way. I guess when you've seen your parents happy in a conventional marriage, you've got to believe that they had something great going for them.

Women on the professional circuit are trying more and more to have an appealing, feminine image. And succeeding. Up to now we've not been able to match the appeal men's golf has had for so long but we're getting there. What with exciting new players, who don't settle for pars and bogeys but who are constantly aiming for birdies, and television coverage and all, we're drawing big galleries and very substantial prize money compared to just a few years ago. And one of the factors is that, as a crowd, I think we look really nice and feminine. For a while a short time back there were only two especially glamorous-looking lady golfers, Laura Baugh, who is a real beauty, and Jan Stephenson, who is mighty sexy-looking. Two in a whole field was hardly enough to make women's golf really interesting in this respect, but now there's a whole bunch of really pretty, or interesting-looking women, who dress attractively and altogether give the pictorial element of watching women's golf a real boost. And the whole thing—the combination of superior golf with the showmanship—has paid off. My own official money winnings of about $200,000 might not stack up to the leading men's money winnings of the year, Tom Watson's approximately $350,000, or to what the top women in tennis have been earning but, as some-

Laura Baugh

Jan Stephenson

body put it, it sure ain't hay. What's more, another half dozen women golfers behind me on the list won something just over or under $100,000 each, and there were a flock of players who piled up between $50,000 and $100,000, so you can't say we're not making a real dent in the sports world. That money, of course, is just prize money for official LPGA tournaments and doesn't include the very considerable extras that are earned through unofficial tournaments, endorsements, or whatnot. I think I can say with safety that women's championship golf has not only come to stay but that it's sure to keep growing all the way from here on in.

One of the things that makes watching us particularly pleasurable for the galleries, both women and men, is our clothes. We are dressed most attractively and we care about how we look for several reasons. Apart from the most natural one of simply caring, a practical one is that many of us have contracts with top clothing companies to wear and display their products. Mine is with Fila, an Italian apparel manufacturer who also specializes in tennis and ski wear— Björn Borg wears Fila tennis shirts. Now the company has entered the golf-apparel field and I'm their first representative. It's exciting because I not only get to wear great clothes but I've also been invited to try my hand at design, which really turns me on. I've got ideas for all sorts of women's looks and figures. I myself simply wear a nice shirt along with either a skirt or pants. I'm very comfortable in pants but prefer a skirt in very hot weather. I don't think I look good in shorts because I'm not slender enough, although when I was much younger and really skinny, I loved shorts. But they're not for me today. I'll try designing them for great figures like Janie Blalock's. Shorts and her former pigtails were Janie's trademarks on the course. But as a matter of fact, what you wear from the waist down isn't that important as far as playing golf is concerned, so you just ought to wear what feels good and makes you look good. The important thing is your shirt, because the most beautiful shirt in the world is no good if it constricts your swing at all and doesn't allow you complete freedom. Luckily, a fine golf shirt can be both beautiful and completely practical.

People sometimes ask me if the wearing of jewelry is any distraction when I play. I don't find it so at all and it makes me feel extra feminine which I guess you know I like by this time. So I wear necklaces and bracelets all the time and never give them a thought when I'm out on the golf course. It's my impression that's true of all of us women and it seems to be true of lots of men athletes as well, even in

Jane Blalock

much more active sports like track and field, or basketball. You see guys with gold pendants dangling from their necks all the time on TV, clearing a high-jump bar or going to the basket for a slam-dunk.

There is one thing that would substantially increase the popular interest in women's golf in the future, I think, if it could be effected. As of now, the tour goes on week after week throughout the golfing year but, with a couple of exceptions, one tournament isn't that distinguishable from another to make it stand out in people's minds as being a big sporting event. The two exceptions, of course, have been the LPGA (Ladies' Professional Golfers' Association) and the U.S. Open championships. They get fine coverage and exposure.

Well, two such tournaments in a year isn't enough. We ought to build up at least two more that can enjoy a similar sort of prestige, the way men's golf has its four major tournaments, the U.S. Open, the British Open, the PGA championship, and the Masters. Each of these carries a particular excitement for golf fans, and winning any of them means much more than winning a tournament named after a city or a movie celebrity even if such events pay off with a big purse. That's forgotten the following week, but anyone who wins one of the majors goes down in golfing history and is remembered. And the idea of somebody, some day, making a Grand Slam sweep of all four in one year is one of the very big things that could ever be achieved in the world of sport. It's never been done, although Ben Hogan and Jack Nicklaus both came close. The one and only Grand Slam, Bobby Jones's in 1930, was a great performance but the conditions were completely different then, with two of the four tournaments he won being amateur events.

Well, women should have a goal like that and, even if a Grand Slam for any of us would be just as unlikely as it is for the men players, at least we'd have four times when a tournament would have real meaning and prestige, instead of only two. With that in mind, a real effort was made to inaugurate a Ladies' Masters at Moss Creek on Hilton Head Island, South Carolina. But the people at Augusta, the site of the original Masters tournament, felt they had an exclusive on the name "The Masters" and were, perhaps justifiably, jealous of having anyone else share it. They won their case, so now our tournament is called the Women's International. But even with that second choice of name I think that's an event that could be built up to be the third major for women, because the entry list is invited much as the Masters is, and all the right players will be in it each year. The recent good news is that over last winter the Peter Jackson Classic, a Canadian tournament, has been designated a "major event" carrying big money prizes. So that constitutes a third big one, and meanwhile we do have as another possibility the well-established Colgate's European, which I won at Sunningdale. It could turn into a sort of an equivalent of the British Open for men.

There's one good thing about championship women's golf. It is on its way up like a shooting star, and there's a lot of room for it to reach for, up into the stratosphere!

Chapter 4

A Computer Between the Ears

My Education in Mathematics and Physics

I'VE TOLD YOU that math was my best subject in school. I never found much use for things like algebra or trigonometry once I got out of the classroom and onto the golf course, but you have a lot of reason to pay attention to numbers. Come to think of it, practically everything in golf is run by the numbers.

Take as an example just starting out to play a round in a tournament. You're not allowed to carry any more than fourteen clubs in your bag. That may seem to you more than enough but the fact is that if you had one of every number given to clubs, you'd definitely have more than fourteen. Just to take the most common clubs, and golf manufacturers actually offer even more than these, you'd have four woods, numbered 1 to 4, and then ten irons, ranging from a 1 (the driving iron) to a 10 (the sand wedge). That adds up to fourteen, but what are you going to use when you get onto the green? The sand wedge? No, you need a putter too, so now you're going to have to get rid of one of those other fourteen clubs or you'll be in trouble. What sort of trouble? Bad trouble. In match play, you forfeit any hole on which you carried more than fourteen clubs. In medal play, you are penalized two strokes per hole. The fact that there's a limit to your penalty, two holes in match play and four strokes in medal, is very small consolation if it ever happens to you. I'm mighty glad it never has to me, because losing four strokes in one round of a tournament, for no real reason at all, is an almost impossible handicap to make up.

So you've got to be careful. Professional golfers are sure to accumulate extra clubs as a matter of course, and it's only natural to try them out in practice sessions. Then you may forget to check and see you have no more than fourteen in your bag when you put the bag back into a locker, or stash it into the trunk of your car. Next time out you may overlook making a count. You shouldn't, and of course a good caddie would always check your bag, but every caddie isn't necessarily a good caddie. Or maybe he's not necessarily a good counter. In any case, if you do goof it's your fault and there's no appealing the injustice of any penalty to the committee or, for that matter, the Supreme Court. Judgment decisions, such as what constitutes casual water, can be made, but the basic rules of golf are inflexible, and a good thing too. It's one of the things that makes golf such a wonderful game. You *know* where you stand and there's never any argument. Tell me another sport that can say that.

Another time numbers come into the picture is on your scorecard when a figure—I hope a very low one—is penciled in under your name after each hole is played, and then all eighteen numbers totaled at the end of the round. Once again, and even more importantly, the need to be mathematically meticulous is a vital part of championship golf. I'm not talking about lying or cheating on your score. That simply doesn't happen in professional circles and I hope it doesn't in yours either. I'm talking about a stupid clerical error, or a bum job of addition that makes your scorecard even the tiniest bit inaccurate. If that happens, no matter how innocent your intentions, or how meaningless the result in giving you an advantage over what the proper scoring should have been, you are automatically disqualified from that tournament and can pack your bag and go home and wait for the next one. In the other case, you suffer a penalty that may seem unfair. The two classic cases in our time involved a great woman golfer, Jackie Pung of Hawaii, and a decade later, a great man golfer, Roberto de Vicenzo of Argentina.

You see, in a tournament a golfer doesn't put down his or her own official score on the card. Let's say I am playing with JoAnne Carner and Judy Rankin. Judy might give her scorecard to JoAnne, JoAnne hers to me, and I'll give mine to Judy. All the way around the full eighteen holes my chief scoring job is to keep JoAnne's score, but in the end it's going to be her responsibility to check it and see that it's right. Hole by hole, as well as the total, and it's all got to be settled between us before we each sign our cards which says, once and for all, "That's it."

Well, in Jackie Pung's case, her scorer accidentally credited her on one hole with a score one stroke lower than she actually made on that hole, but that error was swallowed up in everyone's mind along the way because all concerned were accurately up to date on what Pung's total score was, and what she needed to do on the final holes to win this Women's Open. She came through, seemed to have the tournament won, and her *total* score on the card she signed was the correct one. So it really made no difference that her scorer had penciled in an incorrect figure on one particular hole, because the error had been completely unimportant and had been compensated for in the only thing that mattered, the total. However . . . tough luck, Jackie! I've heard there was a lot of disagreement at the time about enforcing the rules so strictly (I've only heard because it took place the year I was born), but Jackie Pung did not go down as the winner of the 1957 Championship although she actually won. Betsy Rawls did, which is at least some consolation for those who know and care about women's golf. Because if Jackie Pung was so unlucky, at least the one who benefitted was Betsy. Betsy has always shown every good quality being the great champion she was for so many years, as well as being universally admired as an outstandingly fine person.

The de Vicenzo case was similar, but not quite the same. His scorer marked him as having scored one stroke *more* than he actually shot on a hole in the last round. Once again everybody knew de Vicenzo's correct total, and that right figure was properly written at the bottom of his card. If it had been made official, it would have tied him with Bob Goalby for the 1968 Masters championship and would have necessitated a play-off. But in this case, since the math error gave de Vicenzo one stroke *more* than the actual score he shot, he wasn't disqualified. All that happened to him was plenty. The higher (incorrect) score was the one credited to him, and that one shot extra obviously dropped him out of the tie he had earned and gave the title to Goalby.

Do you see what I mean about golf? Numbers, numbers, numbers. Despite a certain cockiness I have about being accurate in marking a scorecard and adding it up, I'll sometimes check mine as many as five times before signing, and never any less than three times. While we're playing we are all apt to be thinking about nothing but our total scores, but when I sit down at the scorer's table I go over each hole, one by one. I guess my memory is as good as the next person's when it comes to remembering names and addresses and telephone numbers and stuff like that, but perhaps no better. But when it comes to recalling each and every shot of a round I've just played, I think I'd be ready to testify in court just what the shot was, and what club I used, and what happened. Nor do I believe I'm particularly unusual in that because it seems to me that just about every professional golfer, being interviewed in the press tent after a round, is able to discuss such details with complete confidence. Call it a golfer's secondary characteristic, like calluses on certain fingers.

What else? Well, of course there are eighteen holes on a regulation course, and a par that's usually 72 or a stroke or two one side or the other of it. Call it 72 because that's par on more courses than any other figure and because it makes the mathematics that follow neater. Eighteen holes, par-72, that means an average of four strokes per hole. If every hole were the same length, a 6,000-yard course (most women's events involve a yardage in the low 6,000's) would see eighteen consecutive holes, each measuring a little under 350 yards. On a 7,000-yard course, which is closer to the men's championship distance, we'd see the same except that then each hole would be a little under 400 yards. In either case, a top woman or man should be able to go around in even 4's without much trouble. Some dreary pair of courses I've dreamed up, haven't I? Luckily golf architects are more imaginative.

For it isn't distance alone that distinguishes one golf hole from another, or makes one easier or harder, but variety of distances certainly does. So a typical golf course will be laid out, let's say, with a dozen par-4's of varying distances, and if some are shorter than my dull theoretical averages given above they're not that much easier to score birdies upon than if they were somewhat longer. But, on those holes that compensate in the other direction, and run 50 yards or so longer than the average lengths quoted, that's the sort of thing that separates the men from the boys, the women from the girls. Because for a woman to score consistent pars, to say nothing of birdies, on 400-yarders, or for men to do so on 450-yarders, takes doing!

In like fashion, the other six holes are apt to consist of three par-3's and three par-5's, to make up the grand total of a par-72. Here again is a stimulating opportunity to get away from Nancy's boring string of comparatively easy par-4's, and champions make the most of the par-3 holes and even more particularly of the -5's. Most tournament winners are made, and losers broken, on those holes, and probably one of the several reasons is because they loom as substantially different from the more routine par-4's. You're forced to break out of what may have become an easy pattern of play. Still, we are talking numbers in this chapter, and it's a little interesting to observe that, disregarding the other factors that may make a course particularly difficult, the imaginary uniform eighteen par-4's course should be a cinch to score 72 upon, whereas a true course, with a dozen long and short -4's and three -3's and three -5's of varying distances, always presents a challenge to match par. Even for the best. And yet those two courses (one of which, happily, doesn't exist except in my imagination) would require you to take a set of clubs and cover exactly the same total distance. While there may be nothing to be learned from this excursion into the subtleties of the lengths of golf holes, and perhaps not much point, mathematically it's a little interesting that given the same numbers (length of course and number of holes) it makes

such a fantastic difference, not only in the interest of playing the game of golf, but in the results. Admittedly I am
guessing what the results would be on my all-4's course, but
I'm pretty sure I'm right and that any golfer would agree.

To push on along into the numbers game, I've already
pointed out in the chapter about my philosophy that a long
seventy-two hole tournament holds comforts along the way
for a player who has run into some trouble but who has
confidence in herself. Time is on her side, for she figures
that misfortune or lapses will average out in the course of
each player taking nearly three-hundred strokes, and that
the cream will eventually rise to the top. But I do think that
the great difference today between the attitude that women
golfers have, and what they used to have, is that they are
not trying to avoid bogeys, as they once did, but rather they
are reaching out for birdies whenever they can, and being
perhaps even a bit disappointed when a possible birdie
backs up into being a par. Four 72's in a tournament for a
total of 288 is admittedly good enough, even today, to win
most women's tournaments, but it isn't always good enough
by any means, and it's not my psychological goal. I think
"birdie" whenever I think I have a chance, and only partly
because one has to do so in order to balance the inevitable
occasional bogey, or worse. Considerably more important
is keeping that charging, right frame of mind. "Par" is obviously the basic goal on each hole, but it's more just there
as a foundation in the back of my mind. "Birdie!" springs
to the forefront of my mind whenever there's an opening.
(Perhaps that is my education in ornithology.) One of the
most flattering things that's ever been said about my golf is
that it reminds some people of Arnold Palmer's game in his
heyday. (And not just because we're both supposed to have
bad swings!) Palmer's mottoes were "Charge!" and "Go for
Broke!" and I not only think he had the right idea for win-

A vital putt that dropped on the way to my winning my fifth straight tournament

ning, but also the right idea for maximum fun. Maybe that philosophy isn't best for everyone, and there certainly have been many successful golfers much more conservatively minded, but believing you can do anything and taking a stab at it worked for Palmer, and so far it has for me.

Our next math lecture has to do with clubs—not the maximum number of fourteen that we've covered before, but how and why they are named—by the numbers.

Years ago golf clubs used to have rather sweet names that had personality, like "spoon" and "midiron" and "mashie" and "niblick." But all that is long in the past, and scientific know-how came up with the "matched set" of golf clubs, which is perhaps less romantic but ever so much better for good golf. Certainly it is for the game I learned to play, and if I've missed something by not experiencing the greater variety of touch and style of play of the old days, which I don't deny may be the case, I don't regret it. For today, as long as I estimate the yardage I need to cover correctly, I can just pick the right club out of my bag that I know will do the trick and, with exactly the same swing as I'd make with a different club for a different distance, consistently bang a ball up onto the green and, it is to be hoped, close enough to the pin to give me a chance for a birdie putt. I really don't have to consider anything much except to perform that swing properly. Sure, I will take wind and weather and the condition of the course into some account, but essentially I can rely upon the fact that, for example, if I have a 150-yard shot to the green, my stroke with a 7-iron will be just right.

Now that sure simplifies life. If I had a grab-bag collection of clubs, picked up here and there as I understand all golfers in Bobby Jones's time acquired their clubs, there would be a lot of other complications in deciding how to play that 150-yard shot. I might not like the weight and balance of that 7-iron (then called a mashie niblick) for a full swing, keeping it primarily for short pitches, and I might feel more comfortable selecting my 5-iron (a mashie, to Bobby Jones) and sparing the shot. That sort of shot-making must have been interesting in a way, but it's not golf as it's played today and it's not for me. I have nothing but gratitude for what's been done to make clubs effective. In a matched set, the "swing weight" that I mentioned earlier, and said I didn't understand too well, is the factor that tries (and succeeds) in making all the irons in a matched set feel the same to you, as you swing one after another. As I get it, in "simple" terms swing weight is the distribution of weight along a golf club, from grip end to clubhead, keyed to a static balance system. (Those are the simplest terms I was able to boil my scientific informant's long descriptions down to, and if I passed along all he said you wouldn't dig it any better than I was able to. Little spots swam before my eyes, so I'll spare you.)

Anyhow, I've indicated that the swing weight I favor is D-1, and the reason I bring it up again is to let you appreciate still another aspect of the role of numbers in the golf business. For I know that there are A, B, C, D, and E swing weights, and while I've never heard of them I wouldn't be too amazed to learn that the letters run right through the alphabet to the letter Z, but I hardly think that's possible. The real point here is that each of these letters is followed by a number: Each letter is broken up into increments of 10. So in a golf club manufacturer's catalogue, my D-1 set of matched clubs would have a little heavier swing weight than a C-10, and a little lighter than a D-2. Talk about introducing the metric system into the country! Seems to me it's already here. Or I guess that's maybe more like what I remember of decimals. Tens, right?

Let's go back to those fourteen clubs you have in your bag, or maybe more if you're not competing seriously and are casually not paying attention to the rule. Of course, each club including your woods actually bears a number on it, from 1 on up, and each higher number indicates that the clubface has a bit more loft. The face of a number 1 is nearly perpendicular to the ground, and each succeeding higher number sees the face laid back more and more, which affords less distance but a higher arc of shot. As the numbers increase, the shaft also becomes a little shorter but that constant old devil, swing weight, stays the same as the result of the magic the club-makers work, so that in a matched set a short club with a heavy head actually swings and feels just like the longer club with a lighter head. Peace, it's wonderful!

Of course, when you think about mathematics in the modern world, the word is that it's the bottom line that counts. In the case of us pro golfers, the bottom line is the prize money plus whatever else we manage to earn or get tossed at us as a result of golfing success. The fact of the matter is that the more money I've made on the professional circuit, the more expensive gifts I've been receiving. I'm certainly not complaining about that, but I guess there's enough to say about it all that it really belongs in another part of this book. That would be the chapter about my education in business, and that will be along a little later.

Chapter 5
Life and Death on the Fairway

My Education in Psychology

IN MANY WAYS, the personal lives of women professional golfers evoke as much public curiosity as how we hit our fairway wooden clubs. I suppose that's true of all performers, whether they're movie stars or rock music artists or golfers, and I guess curiosity is a natural human trait. I'll admit I have my share of it, so I'm going to do my best to tell you a few things about our group, but I'd better warn you at the beginning. Nothing here is going to be excerpted for use in a sensational sex magazine for three reasons. The first is that if I did know something juicy in that respect about one of my golf rivals, the chances are she'd be a friend and I'd have no temptation at all to print gossip about her. The second reason is an even better one. I'm not so innocent that rumors never reach my ears, but out of my own personal knowledge I really don't know anything very titillating to tell you. The final reason is the clincher, at least to me. The whole thing is none of my business.

Probably you sense the topic to which I'm referring, since it invariably is whispered about with any group of women whose job has them traveling together. As a group I really like the women on the tour, and as individuals I really love a few. I love my father and sister and Tim too, each in a different way, and none of those ways even suggests lesbianism. So let's put down that ghost here briefly, once and for all. The offensively prying will maintain that lesbian relationships exist among any group like ours, whether it be in another sport, or the theater, or the dance, or whatever. Maybe so, but if it exists I'm not aware of it, and if I were I'd consider it their concern alone. The fact is that most of us who do well financially on the tour, including me, room alone and don't even go out much, even to dinner, during a tournament. So the tour is not exactly saturnalia. The women who are not doing as well may share accommodations sometimes to save money, but throwing mud at them for that reason makes as much sense as throwing mud at any girl who chooses to live in a YWCA because it's cheap. The things that are really cheap are the insinuations, and I've had enough of discussing it even this much.

Nor will I say much more about the other private female topic that the tastelessly nosy raise sometimes, the effect of a woman's monthly menstruation on her golf. Of course it has an effect, a great deal with some women and less with others, and there's no doubt that there are times when a player who is having a good streak comes up with an inexplicably bad round and that's the reason. Incidentally, a medical friend has told me that occasionally it can work the other way, and that certain women reach their physical peaks just before their periods arrive. In their cases it would be smart of them to be sure to play in a tournament when their periods were due to come on the Monday after the event! I don't know about that, but I certainly am sure that lots of women find that playing their best golf during menstruation is virtually impossible.

We women golfers are all in the same business—one that goes on and on for months on end in a close association of interest—so a natural set of relationships develops. It can range from solid companionship and friendliness to rivalries and jealousy, I suppose. I happen to be something more of a loner than many others, so my own reactions to people on the tour are apt to be less intense than a few of the more gregarious. However, for what insight it may give you, here is how I feel about certain personalities, and the games of some of my major opponents. I'm taking them up alphabetically, both for diplomacy's sake and because it allows me to begin with one of the most interesting and talented of the girls, my good friend,

Amy Alcott. I like Amy particularly, I guess, because I feel an identification of sorts with her. She has been one of the forerunners of the "Youth Movement" of the LPGA of the past couple of years, of which I'm a member in good standing. Amy is a year older than I and she won the same

Amy Alcott

Rookie-of-the-Year award that I did but at a younger age. Today she's one of our top players, and her 70 over the tough Pebble Beach course is the women's record. She's a very outgoing person, not at all reluctant to tell anyone exactly how she feels, about anything at all, without any embarrassment. I like that, and I believe I'm a little like that too. Amy's game is particularly impressive on iron shots. She punches them the way the best men pros do, sending the turf flying, even on pitches as short as forty yards, and that aspect of her game won her the vote as "the best striker of the ball" at the Colgate European at Sunningdale. Although I won that one, the best thing that was said about me as I left the last green as the champion was that I was "still in a cocoon of concentration as if in a trance."

Debbie Austin. Debbie is a little bit older, having turned professional back in 1968 after a fine amateur career. Then she went through nine years, often finishing well up near

Debbie Austin

the top but never winning a tournament. It was incredible, for she was too good a golfer and competitor for that to be happening, but it did. Then finally she won at Birmingham in 1977 and, with that one win finally under her belt, she knocked off four more tournament wins in quite rapid succession! She had almost quit the tour earlier in the year but it's great that she didn't, for Debbie is a lively, friendly person who is liked and admired both by the galleries and those who know her well. I can't claim that we're intimate friends but we're good casual ones.

Laura Baugh. Although, sadly, she's never won a pro tournament, you can't overlook Laura when you run down the list of top or interesting women golfers. She was a brilliant teen-age amateur star and was enticed into turning professional by being able to sign up for more endorsement money than anyone had seen up to that point. That was because Laura is an absolutely stunning beauty in addition to her golf skills, and she can make a great advertisement

Laura Baugh

for any feminine product. For a while I understand people on the tour resented her (it was before my day), but that isn't the case now, nor has it been for a long time. For Laura's personality is as good as her looks and both have done a lot to make women's golf interesting and alluring. But I do feel that her assets may have turned into a liability for her in a golfing sense. She's never turned out to be the golfer she might have been, although she practices conscientiously, and I suspect that she may have been tempted to play upon her looks, rather than her game, and the latter suffered. I like to look attractive and feminine too, but I know that once out upon the course you've got to go all out, and work and sweat when it's necessary. I'm not sure Laura has been prepared to do that all the way, and what I say is only critical in a golf sense. It's Laura's decision what her priorities are and very possibly she knows best. She sure is a knockout!

Silvia Bertolaccini comes originally from Argentina, but she now lives in Dallas. I don't know her very well, and although we've played golf together a few times, I couldn't claim we were more than acquaintances. Our closest bond is that when my Dad can manage to come and be with me when a tournament's going on, Silvia and Dad chat with

Silvia Bertolaccini

each other a lot in Spanish. She is a darned good golfer who doesn't hit the long ball but makes up for it by the extreme intelligence and skill with which she places the ball. She won the Colgate Far East Open in 1977, the year before I did, and she took the Civitan Open last October. I rate her a really solid golfer.

Jane Blalock. I really like Janie. She has a great sense of humor and you can joke around with her. And I really love to play golf with her because she's such a fighter. You can see that fighting instinct in her every movement around the course. She really works *so* hard to get every putt in, and that's a big part of it, but she's aggressive all the way. Janie

Jane Blalock

is a little older than some of us and has been a pro about ten years now, during which time she's piled up one of the really top records. She is very frank and outspoken about anything she feels keenly about, which is a characteristic I particularly admire. You used to be able to spot her in any tournament, with her shorts and her pigtails, but she's given up the pigtails now. Anyhow the thing that really distinguishes her is that she's got guts.

Pat Bradley. A very quiet girl who prefers to keep to herself. Despite that, we've been very good friends since I joined the tour. Pat's a fine golfer who's getting better all the time, in the face of being set back severely by a hand injury a couple of years ago. I understand she was once a big, wild hitter of the ball, but you'd never know it now. She modified her game and today she plays more for intelligent, consistent, even "safe" golf. But she's a whiz with a long iron when the situation calls for it. I admire her a lot, both as a golfer and a person.

Pat Bradley

Jerilyn Britz

Jerilyn Britz is one of the older women pros and maybe that's why we've never been too close. She is all business when she's out on the course, which is good. She didn't play serious golf too much until recent years, but even so she qualified for the Colgate Triple Crown event this year, and I'll admit that was the reason I included her on this list originally. But there's a much better reason now. At the last moment left for me to sneak some late news into this book, Jerilyn won her first tournament ever. And what was it? Nothing less than the biggest one of all—the U.S. Womens Open! Congratulations, Jerilyn. It was a super performance!

JoAnne Carner. Now we're talking about one of the really great ones. As JoAnne Gunderson she had the best record any amateur ever achieved before turning professional, which she did back in 1970. Always a tough fighter, she was a super match player, and most amateur events are match play affairs. As a pro, she's consistently been a top-notcher, and continues to dominate match play events when they're held. I literally idolized her when I was an amateur and

JoAnne Carner

now, playing against her on even terms, I still kind of do. She has the sort of personality that I wanted to have when I came onto the tour. She seemed to make every shot exciting, from the long ones right down to the putts. The crowds like her very much—*exciting* is really the right word for her. She has very individual mannerisms on the putting greens that bother some of the players partnered with her, but the gallery likes to watch her and she really turns the gallery on when she drives! She hits the ball with the arm and hand action of a man and she often achieves distances off the tee like 275 yards. Since she's mighty good at everything else too, there's a school of thought that believes JoAnne ought to hang her head in shame any time she doesn't win a tournament played over a long course, because she outdrives almost everybody else by so much. I'm a long driver myself, but I'm not sure I'd like to get into a driving contest for big money against JoAnne. Still I do remember one time when JoAnne was leading the tournament going into the last day. She said she "was going to leave me in the dust." I actually knew it was probably a joking phrase but I purposely pumped myself up and made myself angry, and psychologically it did me good. Because when we each got out on the course to play that final round, I was glad that I was playing in the group right in front of JoAnne, so that she was able to see every shot I made and everything I was doing. I was so charged up that day! I was going to beat her if it was the last thing I ever did! So every time I made a good shot, I would just kind of turn around and look to see if she was watching, which she generally was. She had put pressure on me, perhaps unintentionally, but now it had boomeranged and I was putting the pressure back on her. That day proved to me something I quietly had always known about myself. Pressure makes me play better—it makes me more aware. Anyhow, Jo-

Anne did not leave me in the dust. I caught her and passed her and won. We've laughed about it together since then, although my laugh was probably more sincere. But JoAnne is such a brilliant shot-maker and fighter that whenever she loses, put a bet down on her next time. I don't know any of my chief rivals I respect more.

She's married to Don Carner, who follows the tour regularly. They travel together in a plush trailer and they keep pretty well to themselves when JoAnne isn't playing. Tim and I have recently bought a trailer ourselves, and maybe we'll be like that too one of these days. But first Tim has his own career to think about.

Dot Germain hasn't made it really big yet as a pro, but like Jerilyn Britz, the fact that she qualified for the Colgate Triple Crown means that she has to be good. Dot's a really good friend of mine and I'm glad to see that she's playing better now than she ever has. She's very accurate when she's on her game, and if she can consistently put together the scores she sometimes pulls off, she's going to win her share.

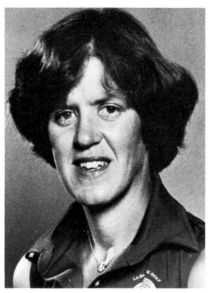

Dot Germain

Chako Higuchi

Chako Higuchi. Chako has the reputation of being the closest thing to a foreign superstar, having dominated womens' golf in Japan for almost ten years. She won three Japanese LPGA and Open titles and then started coming to the United States to compete in at least part of the tour—usually in the early spring events, since that's not tournament season in Japan. She had great years in 1976 and 1977, winning the Colgate European Open the first of those years and taking our LPGA Championship the next year. That was before I turned professional myself, so it wasn't until 1978 that I had a chance to see and meet Chako in competition. She only competed in nine events and she didn't make out quite as well as she had in the two previous years, but it was very clear that here was indeed an international superstar and, even as I'm finishing writing this book in early 1979, she's been proving it again in this country, finishing well up in just about every tournament she enters.

Chako is a big hit with the galleries wherever she plays,

and there are several reasons for it. For one thing her dainty Oriental appearance charms people right from the start and then, despite the wonderful results she gets, her completely unorthodox swing makes any golf analyst first shudder, and then marvel. On her backswing, she sways her body more to the rear than to any good player I've ever seen, but her steady rhythm and timing somehow see to it that her club comes into the ball just right at the moment of impact. She doesn't hit a long ball compared to some of us, and often uses a wood for a medium-long approach to a green where most would take an iron, but her woods usually fly straight as an arrow and land well placed on the green. So the combination of Chako's looks and personality, added to the fascination of watching her unique game, gives any tournament in which she plays an extra attractive touch.

Sally Little is a native-born South African who now lives permanently in Dallas. What is it about Dallas? You'll remember that's the city that also appealed to another foreigner, Silvia Bertolaccini of Argentina. Maybe they ought

Sally Little

to move the United Nations there. Just by chance, I seem to be drawn in a playing group that includes Sally quite often. I'm glad when it happens because Sally has everything that goes towards making a good golfing companion. Like JoAnne Carner, she's a long driver and a fighter, and that means you can't play lazy when Sally is around. She keeps quietly intent upon her own game and never does anything to distract another player. Add to that the fact that she is one of the most attractive-looking women on the tour, always prettily groomed and dressed, and there's little more that need be said about why it's pleasant to find we're in a threesome together. We're not really close friends off the course, but I like her and sense that she likes me.

Carol Mann has been around longer than most of us and her playing record over the years is one of the best in women's golfing history. A marvelous short-iron and bunker player, she is still just about as good as she ever was, despite playing considerably less. One of the best reasons why she chooses not to compete too much anymore is because she's kept so busy these days acting as the LPGA's

Carol Mann

spokesperson, analyst, reporter, and television commentator. She's absolutely the best at all of these things. For two years she was president of the LPGA when the organization most needed direction and growth. She supplied the needed qualities and then was instrumental in the brilliant selection of Ray Volpe as our Commissioner. So every woman on the circuit has reason to be grateful for what Carol has brought to our game, and no one is more deserving of being named to the LPGA Hall of Fame than Carol, who was elected in 1977.

Debbie Massey and I played on the Curtis Cup team together as amateurs, and I not only thought the world of her but, when we competed against each other in match play, she sure had my number! We met three times back then, and all Debbie did was to win three of them! So although I've always continued to think Debbie a particularly nice girl and a very close friend, I'm regularly out for blood when and if I come up against her head-to-head in a tour-

Debbie Massey

nament. I've done a lot better as a professional than I did as an amateur against Debbie, but considering what she did to me then, that wouldn't be hard! She turned pro the year before I did and was Rookie of the Year just before me, winning the Mizuno Classic in Japan for her only tournament victory.

Sandra Palmer is another name to reckon with in modern women's golf. Her record speaks for itself. Standing only a shade over 5 feet and weighing not much more than 100 pounds, she nevertheless has become one of golf's most frequent winners and has pulled down more than half a million dollars in prize money. That's saying something when you realize that Sandra, because of her small frame, seldom drives a ball more than 220 yards and is simply physically unable to hit a long fairway wood or iron the distance that some of us can. She has more than made up for it by intense practice and the development of a brilliant short game. She is literally a stick of dynamite and the

Sandra Palmer

spunkiest little figure around. Her intensity on the course gets on some people's nerves but I admire it, and I feel she's a pretty good friend of mine, even though she's likely to tease me about anything and everything.

Sandra Post is a very consistent and sound stroker of the ball, who bounced into notice with a bang in her very first year as a professional by beating the great Kathy Whitworth in a playoff for the LPGA Championship. That was, in a way, her high point, but she's done very well ever since, winning the Colgate Far East event one time and the Colgate Dinah Shore affair on another, and she's knocked off better than a quarter of a million dollars of official money over her career. I can't really say we're good friends, but I'm not quite sure why. I know her and she knows me, but all we sort of do is to say "Hi!" or "Bye!" as we pass each other. I certainly don't feel that we've anything against each other, but that's the way it is. Chemistry?

Penny Pulz is another foreigner who came to stay in the United States, but who managed to find another city on the map other than Dallas. Not a bad one at all, as a matter of fact—Palm Springs. After a fine amateur career in Australia, she came here to join the tour, and while she's not yet won a U.S. pro tournament, she's been moving up toward the top all the time. I think she's a determined player who's got the game to make it. Maybe I'm prejudiced in her favor, because as a person I rate Penny well up among the people I like best.

Judy Rankin. Judy has been one of the most consistently successful players ever to compete on the circuit. Her record for over a decade has been spectacular, and she capped it in 1976 when she became the first woman ever to win $100,000 in one season, and she did that quite early in the year. She finished that season with over $150,000 in prize money tucked into her purse, and the following year she

Sandra Post

Penny Pulz

Judy Rankin

did nearly as well. Her full career earnings of official money are getting up pretty close to the three-quarters-of-a-million-dollar mark. No wonder her husband, "Yippy" Rankin, loves, admires, and appreciates her. Too much for the rest of us, I fear. For Yippy travels every inch of the tour with Judy, and he's out there every step of every round, rooting, cajoling, entreating, suggesting, and sometimes throwing a temper tantrum if something bad happens to Judy. He's inevitably a distraction to everyone else and once, I'm told, he was actually ordered off the course. I wasn't there then but I can believe it for, along with everyone else, I've seen Yippy in action. I think he puts undue pressure on Judy,

Betsy Rawls

even though I can't say that she doesn't seem to thrive on it. Judy and I are not really good friends, and I don't think there's any doubt that Yippy and I are not. I don't feel that any of the women really keenly resent me and my successful rookie year, but I certainly do feel that Yippy does and, as would be natural, that inclines Judy to be on the cool side too. Well, I guess there's no rule that everybody has to love me. I'm not running for any office.

Betsy Rawls. You absolutely can't write a book about modern women's golf without talking about Betsy, even though she hasn't figured strongly in the tournaments in recent years. An LPGA Hall of Fame member since 1960, she was one of the golfers who dominated the game for some twenty years, winning the U.S. Open *four* times. Since 1975, when she became Tournament Director for the LPGA, she's been inspiration, consultant, friend, and den mother for all of us.

Hollis Stacy. Even though she's been a consistently very good golfer ever since she turned pro in 1974, certain people have had a tendency to underrate Hollis and not realize how very good she can be. That is until last year's Open at

Hollis Stacy

Indianapolis, where she came whizzing through a tough field on the last day and won convincingly. We'd all better look out for her every time from now on, even though she surprisingly didn't qualify for the Colgate Triple Crown. I've played with Hollis very often and I think I see echoes of myself in the way she shows she's out to win and isn't going to let anything stand in the way. That's the way I feel when I'm out there, even if it sometimes doesn't work. Hollis is awfully likable, with a swell sense of humor that keeps people laughing. Her nickname is "Spacy Stacy"—I

Jan Stephenson

guess because everything about her, including her golf game, is somewhat unpredictable.

Jan Stephenson. Jan is the other woman golfer aside from Laura Baugh who perhaps is better known as a sex symbol on the tour than as a regular tournament threat. But I don't feel that's accurate. She certainly is an eyeful, with a gorgeous figure that she shows off to best advantage with the clothes she wears, but her features are more cute than beautiful, while Laura is really dazzling. But looking at the other angle, I've always found Jan an extremely good, serious competitor on the course. She was a great junior champion back in her native Australia when she was younger, and she's been a strong factor on our U.S. tour ever since she joined in 1974, when she was Rookie of the Year. Jan's game is a little erratic and she has a reputation as a streak player—you must watch out for her when she's hot. I really don't know her very well personally and except when we're playing together, we've barely seen each other to date. But don't read anything into that. It's just happened that way.

JoAnn Washam

Jo Ann Washam has only had an in-and-out career as a pro up to now although, standing only 5 foot 3 inches and weighing only 120 pounds, she belts the ball a country mile. She is absolutely one of the longest hitters on the tour, and I only wish the rest of her game could match her skill off the tee. That's because I really care about Jo Ann, and consider her one of my two best friends on the circuit. Donna Young is someone who is particularly special for me, but she's enough older that we have a different sort of relationship. Jo Ann is a bit older than I am too, but she's more of a contemporary. We like each other, go out together, and indirectly I have Jo Ann to thank for getting me my regular caddie, Roscoe. But that's another story that comes later.

Kathy Whitworth and *Mickey Wright*. The fact that I'm grouping these two women together is not because they're less significant in my mind than all the others that I've listed separately. That's the last thing from how I feel about them. They are goddesses and my idols. My ambition is to be the Kathy Whitworth or the Mickey Wright of the next

Kathy Whitworth

LPGA

Mickey Wright

dozen years or so. Why don't I separate them? Because their records and their contributions to golf are so close to each other, and so outstanding, that I don't want to single one out as opposed to the other.

Both are really of the generation of golfers just before my own, although both still play top-notch golf and Kathy, who plays more, continues to be a real threat every time out. Mickey just plays now and then, but because of our age differences I've not had the good fortune to get to know either on a really intimate basis. I can only stand off to one side and admire both.

Kathy is the all-time leading money winner. She has won more titles than any other woman—except who? Mickey Wright, of course, who also holds the record for winning the most tournaments in any one year and who won the U.S. Open four times! Like the great Sam Snead among the men, the peculiar and sadly unfair aspect of Kathy's career is that she somehow never managed to win the Open. Both Sam and Kathy won everything else in sight many times, and Kathy has dominated women's golf for a decade or so.

Donna Caponi Young

Donna Caponi Young. The accident that Donna's name ˎ
comes last on this alphabetical list is a happy one, because
I can finish it off in a burst of honest enthusiasm. Donna is
a really great player, about as good as anyone with her short
irons, and she really can bang something like a 4-wood
right onto the green with the best of them. Also, I've always
been very impressed with her extremely slow backswing
and the controlled tempo she maintains through all her
strokes. That's the way I learned to play and that's what I'm
always trying to do when I'm out on the course. Seeing how

well Donna has made out with the technique strengthens my confidence that it's the right system for me, as well as it has proven to be for her.

But most of all Donna's importance to me is personal. I think of her as if she were my older sister. She is just about the same age as my sister, Delma, and she's near at hand while Delma isn't. So I can really sit and talk to Donna and let down my hair. She helped me get started the right way and she's kept being my friend and supporter even as we developed into keen rivals in golf. It has been an ideal relationship for me, and I'm terribly grateful that I fell into it. Donna's husband, Ken, is awfully nice too, and he's a good, warm friend to have. Donna and I have often been battling each other down the stretch, and she wants to win just as much as I do, but that's never remotely touched how we feel about each other. I really love her. To me she's part of my family.

That's the roster of the women who are out there every week through the season trying to take my bread and butter away while I try to do the same to them. Of course there are others as well, but those are the ones who have been looming largest in my mind most of the time up to now, but maybe there'll be a new Rookie of the Year bursting in any day. But to get down to cases, what have my descriptions and opinions about all these golfers got to do with the subtitle of this chapter, "My Education in Psychology"?

Well, while it's true that we usually compete in medal play, where the prime objective is simply to play your own best game and pit it against the course and par, we do have occasional match play tournaments like the important Colgate Triple Crown event, where you battle one opponent after another (assuming you don't get knocked out by somebody right away!). Even more frequent, however, are the many times when you head into the final holes of a medal play tournament with no more than a stroke or two separating the leaders, and when that happens it's likely to turn into a one-to-one fight, just as in match play. Because usually the leaders are scheduled to be playing as the last ones out on the course, and you're either playing right along with your closest rival or, if she's just in front of you or just behind you, within sight of her. You can see what she's doing, and she can see how you're making out. When that happens, your psychology very naturally is likely to change, and the idea of beating So-and-So, and swapping punches with her until you come out ahead, seems to take precedence over your usual objective to just play well and keep shooting for par or a birdie. Maybe it shouldn't happen that way, but it is a human reaction, isn't it? Remember my story about JoAnne Carner's predicting she'd leave me in the dust, and my reaction and the way it worked out? That's what I mean.

I don't want to go into specifics about individual rivals and how I might play one or the other under such circumstances. With some I wouldn't have any notion or idea about psyching them out and with others I might be unfair in my opinions. What's more, just as a matter of self-interest, it wouldn't be too bright of me to tip my hand. Maybe it would backfire on me just the way JoAnne's comment did on her that time.

So perhaps you'd want to do a little detective work of your own. From what I've written, you may in some cases decide that I find certain opponents unflappable, and you'd be right. In others, such as perhaps a player who hits a short ball, or one who's inclined to be conservative and usually lays up with a shot short of the green rather than take a chance and going for it, I may decide to apply the pressure. I'd be even more inclined then to choose the dangerous option, and try to reach the green in a stroke less than she's going to take to reach it. And sometimes it can work the other way. If I know my rival hits a long ball but is apt to be wild and stray off line, I might play position golf myself looking for the certain par, and try to sucker her into taking the chances. But I'd only be likely to do that when I'm up against someone who I feel is playing against the percentages when she overextends herself.

You know that, by and large, I prefer to take the first shot and try to do so well with it that the challenge is thrown at my opponent to match it or beat it. But if it works out the other way, and she shoots first and pulls off a beauty, that's when I really try to dig in my hardest. Either way, if a fighter or a scrambler (and I think I'm both) pulls the fat out of the fire unexpectedly and accomplishes a comeback shot, it's really likely to take the steam out of her opponent, who thought she had the hole in hand. It's a reverse psychological pressure and it may be the most satisfying one to pull if it succeeds. Very often it takes the form of sinking a long putt when the other player only has a very short one left. She looks a sure thing for her par, and you look most likely to have to settle for a bogey. But just bang that 15-footer into the cup and her disappointment at being halved on a hole she thought she had won is likely to carry over and have an effect on the next hole as well.

"Gamesmanship" is a term invented years ago by a funny British writer named Stephen Potter. It is described the art of winning games by psychological means "without actually cheating." Like showing your opponent a doctor's anatomical chart of the human body with all the muscles and tendons wrapped into a knot on a backswing, and letting him brood about what that might do to that pain that already bothers him in the lower back. Gamesmanship in less exaggerated form can crop up among certain casual weekend golfers, but it's not a part of our sort of serious and really moral, sportsmanlike professional golf. If we ever resort to psychology, it's in a choice of legitimate tactics with our clubs. The game is the thing—not gamesmanship. That's for sure.

Chapter 6

Win Some, Lose Some

My Education in Philosophy

THERE ARE A COUPLE of famous lines of verse that apply—
or should apply—to all sports in a way, although they've
been connected in people's minds to sportsmanship in tennis. That's because a neatly lettered sign has hung for years
over the passage along which the players walk to the center
court on their way to a championship match. The familiar
words read:

> For when the One Great Scorer comes to
>   write against your name—
> He marks—not that you won or lost
>   —but how you played the game.

The point obviously was that playing any game fairly and
with grace is the main idea of it all, but I think there's also
a second and unique meaning peculiar to the game of golf
alone. That interpretation is one of the firmest foundations
of my philosophy about winning and losing, even if the
poet had no such aim in mind. I'll try to explain.

First of all, and this is the lesser aspect of the idea, most of our tournaments are medal play, and the sound way to play such tournaments is not with the idea of beating or losing to someone, as in a match play, but essentially just to do the very best one can over the course. In other words, unless you're down to the final holes in a head-to-head scoring duel with someone, or engaged in a sudden death playoff, your real aim is to do as well against Old Man Par as you can. If you can beat him, you'll do okay, and if somebody else beats him even worse than you do, no one should feel very sorry for you, including yourself. That's the first angle I have about this subject but it's a very general one that, once taken in, hardly ever need be thought about again.

The second angle is more sophisticated and more important, and a good competitor should always be aware of it. Golf is, I believe, the only game where the admittedly very best player over a stretch of time hasn't any more than a pretty good chance of winning any individual golf tournament. He or she may be a comparatively very strong favorite, and a considerably better bet to win than anyone else, but even the greatest golfer, male or female at any time in history, is not a good risk to bet on at anything less than something like 5-to-1 odds against. There are always too many almost equally talented golfers in the field of a major tournament, any one of whom is capable over a given long weekend of putting together four steady or superb rounds, for even the admittedly dominant player in the long run to be favored strongly. That's not true of other sports. A very good tennis player doesn't beat a player of world championship class, or the best fighter at the local gym doesn't unexpectedly knock out the heavyweight champion. (Even Rocky in the movie didn't!) But in golf tournament after tournament, usually there are half a dozen players right up in the lead or within a stroke or two of the leader, over the final nine holes, and any of them can win. The solid favorite, who will far outstrip the person who beats her over the year in victories and in money earnings, may be quite a way back in that particular tournament and be finishing nowhere. It doesn't take *too* much misfortune to shoot your way out of a tournament with a few unexpected bogeys.

I think Jack Nicklaus made the point best one time. He is quoted as saying that a major golf tournament competitor who wins 20 percent of the events he enters is almost surely the world's best. Think about that rather startling statement. The best performer in this sport of golf is likely *not* to win four out of five times over a 72-hole medal play tournament. No wonder golf has been called "a humbling game"!

If you appreciate and accept that philosophy, that you will win some and will lose some, you've taken a long step toward "playing the game" of golf the right way. Inevitably you're going to lose certain strokes, certain holes, certain championships that you felt you blew, but if your golfing education has left you with the right philosophy about it, in the end you'll win more than your share. It's cause and effect. If a wasted shot or a poor round keeps gnawing away at your mind and spirit, it's going to affect your next shot or your next round. If you don't let it, it won't.

I try to put bad things that have happened to me out of my mind right away. I've two pieces of knowledge that let me do just that, hard as it was at the beginning before my philosophical education took hold. The first is that over so long a stretch as fifty-four or seventy-two holes of golf, similar misfortunes are sure to overtake virtually everyone else. The second is that in so lengthy a competitive stretch, there's plenty of time and opportunity for your skill—or luck for that matter—to have a good chance to take effect and even things out. If you're the best or one of the best, time is on your side, so don't panic. In any case, you can't do anything about spilled milk. All the gnashing of teeth in the world isn't going to change that double-bogey–6 back into the par-4 you should have made, but a couple of birdies will make up for it. About all I do after a bad hole is draw a little fence around the figure on my scorecard, so it won't spill over onto the next hole! When I make a birdie I draw a star. Does that mean I'm superstitious? Sure. Who isn't one way or the other?

The philosophy of "Think Positive" is an essential for winning golf. Of course I'll be regretful if I've shot a 75, let's say, in the first round of a tournament. That's a disappointing score for me, and if I don't do any better from then on, this trip wasn't necessary. But I know from experience that with two or three more rounds to come, I have a decent chance to make up for it. So I don't lie awake that night brooding over that first round, because what I do tomorrow and after that is what should be on my mind. I know that, as opposed to a great many players on the tour, I'm likely to score better on the final round or two than on the early ones. Many of the women players feel extra pressure much more keenly toward the end of an event and it shows up with lost strokes. I'm more often geared the other way. It psyches me up to be heading down the homestretch with a chance of winning, and I welcome the pressure. I never quit on a tournament, even when my early situation makes things look pretty hopeless. Of course it's true that second or third or even something like seventh money is a lot more than if you finish way down the line, and that's certainly a factor in making you want to hang in there, but honestly I think I'm driven by something else. Maybe I believe in miracles, or maybe I don't pay too much attention to the doleful figures on the scoreboard about how I'm making out in comparison with the leaders, but even when any realist would know I was hopelessly out of it, I keep aiming to win until the final putt rattles into the hole and I know for a fact that someone else is going to win that particular tournament. After all, there might be a flood or an earthquake or something, mightn't there? And the round would have to be played over again.

The first thing I do after losing, regardless of whether I lost a close one because of a silly lapse or simply was snowed under by a rival running on a hot streak, is to forget it. I take a look at my calendar and start thinking about where we'll be playing next week, and I'll show 'em then! Remember the lyrics in the song "Many a New Day" from the show *Oklahoma!?* The show was long before my day, but the movie is always being revived and the girl tells about not ever looking back, but always looking ahead. She sings that she never asks an August sky what happened to last July.

That's me, and that's a substantial part of my education in philosophy. For example, let me tell you about what happened in the course of my rookie year on the tour in 1978.

If you're interested enough in me at all to be reading this book, you probably know more or less about the beginning. After a couple of first efforts in tournaments early in the year, in which I predictably did nothing much, I broke into the winner's circle for the first time as a pro in the Bent Tree Classic at Sarasota, Florida. I don't know if winning any other tournament will ever again mean quite as much to me, and not only because it was my first victory. I had just returned to the tour after my Mom's death and somehow, knowing how much she loved me and how much she wanted for me to make good, I became stronger mentally for her sake.

It was a seventy-two-hole tournament and I was well satisfied with my first round 71, but it was only good enough to place me two strokes back of Hollis Stacy's spectacular 69, one back of Betsy King's 70, and in a tie for third with Laura Baugh. Over the next eighteen Hollis, who was going to play so consistently a few weeks later in winning the U.S. Open, blew up to a 78 and shot her way out of this tournament, and Laura did the same. But Betsy reeled off a neat 71, one stroke less than my 72, and took the lead by two strokes. Actually JoAnne Carner's 69 was the day's sensation but that, added to her first round of 76, left her four strokes behind Betsy and two behind me. Donna White and Amy Alcott were right in there too breathing down our necks. The third round in a seventy-two-hole affair is often the one that goes a long way toward settling things, and while Silvia Bertolaccini shot a fine 69 while all of us early leaders were settling for solid but unspectacular rounds in the low 70's, the girl who was really burning up the course was my pal Jo Ann Washam, who posted a 67. So at the end of that third round we were bunched, with Donna White and I in the lead at 216, Jo Ann only one stroke back, Amy Alcott two, and Silvia and JoAnne Carner three strokes off the pace. Anybody's tournament.

But Donna soared to a 76 on the final round while I was shooting a 73, good enough to stand up against all the others, and I had won my first professional tournament. My total was 289, one over par for the four rounds, and while I've played better in tournaments both before and since, that first win at Bent Tree meant more to me emotionally than any other.

When I got the lead in the last round I was absolutely determined not to lose it, and I didn't. I remember crying all the way down the seventy-second fairway, knowing that I had the victory pretty well in hand unless I blew it completely, and I couldn't stop crying right through the award

Sometimes Hollis Stacy congratulates me and sometimes it's the other way around

ceremony, at which I dedicated my win to my mother's memory. No matter what else lies in store for me in golf, Bent Tree will always be something very special.

Right after that, in the next tournament, the Sunstar Classic at the Rancho Park Golf Club in Los Angeles, I won again, and now people started to sit up and take notice of me. A number of newspaper articles and magazine stories about me began to appear and I have to admit that it was fun. Also, I had now won two big-money purses and the Lopez family was beginning to see more money than they had ever seen before. I was starting to repay my Dad's unbounded love and confidence in me, and it would have been perfect if only my dear Mom had been around to share in it all.

But after the Sunstar and the early splash of publicity,

I got a trophy at the Sunstar Classic and Dad got a kiss from runner-up Debbie Massey.

On the check:

sunstar classic
LPGA GOLF CHAMPIONSHIP

Nº 711

March 12 1978

PAY TO THE ORDER OF

THE SUM

Nancy Lopez

Fifteen thousand

$15,000.00

DOLLARS

LA First Los Angeles Bank

Will a bank really cash a check like this?

Jack Nicklaus's percentage theory caught up with me. I kept playing pretty well, but there are a lot of wonderful women golfers on the tour and no one was hanging around waiting for this rookie to walk all over them. In my next five tournaments the best I could do was to finish second in one, the Kathryn Crosby/Honda Civic Classic, but my next best was no better than a tie for fifth, and in one other I finished far down the list in a tie for eighteenth place. Still, life was more than okay. I was having a very gratifying rookie year, with two tournament triumphs already under my belt and prize-money winnings well in excess of $50,000. I really couldn't expect or hope for much more in the half year to go.

What happened next, therefore, might have sprung right out of *Fantasy Stories* or *True Romances*. *I won the next five tournaments IN A ROW*, a feat unmatched in women's golf history. For the record they were:

Greater Baltimore Classic, Pine Ridge C. C., Lutherville, Md.
'78 LPGA Coca Cola Classic, Forsgate C. C., Jamesburg, N.J.,
Golden Lights Championship, Wykagyl C. C., New Rochelle, N.Y.
LPGA Chapionship, Jack Nicklaus G. C., Kings Island, Ohio
Bankers Trust Classic, Locust Hill C. C., Rochester, N.Y.

The big one, of course, was the fourth-in-a-row win, my taking of the LPGA Championship. It was the tournament up to then that carried the greatest prestige and that I wanted dearly to win, and everything came up roses for me over those four days. My first round of 71 wasn't anything exceptional but it was good enough to put me right up there, and the next day when I really got hot with a second round of 65, I guess it became sort of discouraging for everybody else. I had a nine-hole stretch in that round, from the ninth hole through the seventeenth, where I shot eagle, birdie, par, par, birdie, eagle, par, birdie, birdie. Dad called it right when he yelled, some place near the end of that run, "Nancy, that ball got eyes!"

The Coca Cola Classic had a particularly nice and unusual trophy for the winner

I stayed sky high for the final two rounds, shooting a 69 and a 70 for a total seventy-two-hole score of 275 over Jack Nicklaus's 6,312-yard Golf Center Course. That was thirteen strokes under par and left me with a fat six-stroke lead over Amy Alcott, the runner-up. It was just a super tournament for me in every way, being such an important one, having played so well, doing it while my Dad was watching, and keeping my streak of consecutive wins going so that now I'd won four in a row. That tied the record to date shared by Mickey Wright, Kathy Whitworth, and Shirley Englehorn. If I could just win my next tournament, I'd have the record all to myself.

So I headed for the Bankers Trust Classic in Rochester riding high and feeling very determined. But there sure were a lot of distractions throughout the early part of that week. First a golf match for me was arranged where I played with former President Gerald Ford. That was a thrilling experience even if the golf was no better than ordinary.

The next day I went to New York to appear on the *Good Morning America* show on television, and I was bowled over by how many people recognized me right out on the street walking with my manager. Some actually yelled "Good luck!" to me right out of their car windows. Later, when I got back to Rochester and turned on the TV, there I was hitting balls while Carly Simon sang "Nobody Does It Better" as the background. Wow!

We had a day of practice coming up the following morning, and I figured I'd have a chance to settle down a bit before the tournament. But believe it or not, when I showed up at the practice tee, where usually no one is around except the players, several hundred people had turned out just to see me take some swings! I almost had to fight my way through my well-wishers to get to the clubhouse for lunch.

Former President Gerald Ford sinks a putt while Bob Hope and I watch. Can you tell who was his partner from our expressions?

Once the tournament started I played pretty well, but my 72 on the first eighteen could have been a bit better. It was good enough so that I was only one stroke off the pace, but something happened at the beginning of the back nine that really shook me up. My drive went off line from the tenth tee and went into the crowd of spectators lining the fairway some two-hundred yards or more out. And it hit a man named Dr. Jerry Mesolella right on the head. I rushed up there and burst into tears as I saw him lying on the ground with some blood on his forehead. As I reached out to hold his hand he looked up and said to a friend, "At least I'm going to get a chance to meet her!" So he wasn't badly hurt at all, but if he had been I'm sure I would have dropped out, no matter how important the tournament seemed to me. As it was I kept crying all the way along the hole, after Dr. Mesolella said he was okay and waved me on, and I double-bogeyed it, but I pulled myself together then and scored my 72. The next day I had a 73, which didn't make my chances of winning seem too rosy, but in the third and final day of this fifty-four-hole event, I managed to cut loose and banged out a 4-under-par 69. That did it. My total of 214 was good enough to beat Jane Blalock and Debbie Massey by two strokes. At the presentation ceremony I blew a kiss to Dr. Mesolella and thanked him for his encouragement. Everything might have been very different if he'd been a different sort of person, or if he'd happened to have been hurt badly.

So now I had really pulled it off! Five straight tournament wins for a new record, and starting right then I guess I became a real, honest-to-goodness celebrity!

Suddenly I was right up there with all the celebrities, including my own pet celebrity, John Travolta! (I've only seen *Saturday Night Fever* five times but then I'm still just

Dinah Shore, terrific promotor of womens' golf, had me on her talk show, "Dinah!"

twenty-two!) On Sunday, July second, *The New York Times Magazine* splashed my picture all over its front cover, accompanied by a long, first-feature story by Grace Lichtenstein. *Sports Illustrated* followed on July tenth with another color portrait on its cover and a feature article by Frank Deford (even though Barry McDermott had written a major piece about me in the same magazine the previous month, after I had won the LPGA). It seemed that just about every publication in the country, from *Time* and *Newsweek* and, of course, all the major specialized golf magazines, right along the line through the country's newspapers from New York to Podunk, wrote about what they were calling the Wonder Woman. (They lifted that term from an interview with Judy Rankin who said of me, "They've got the wrong Wonder Woman on TV.")

Of course it was tremendously exciting and satisfying to be the center of so much attention and praise and it still is, but I hope it never gives me the big head. I don't think it has yet. After all, I'm still a young girl with not too much to be conceited about except that I can hit a golf ball. That means a lot to me personally, and it seems to mean a lot to a surprisingly big bunch of people, but I do have some perspective about how my God-given talent fits into the cosmic scheme of the universe. I'm grateful, and excited, and pleased and that's all. The hoopla about me probably has done something to bolster my self-confidence in my golf game but, to be honest, I've always had that from the earliest days on the municipal course in Roswell with Dad. I really think I can do almost anything on a golf course within my physical limits if I put my mind to it hard enough, and I'd like to think that is healthy cockiness for a competitor, and not the big head.

As for the people who crowd around to say a few words or to get my autograph, I love them both individually and in a crowd. Part of my philosophy is that a gallery, far from upsetting me, psyches me up. Of course it helps that so far most are rooting for me to do well: It gives me the edge that a hometown crowd gives its team in other sports. It's not only flattering but encouraging to see people wearing "Nancy's Navy" buttons (a takeoff, of course, of Arnold Palmer's famous "Arnie's Army"), but I suspect that my attitude toward autograph seekers shows best how I feel. Some people marvel at how I don't seem annoyed by requests, even when they come at inappropriate times such as walking to the first tee for the final round of a big tournament, but the fact is that I like and appreciate such attention, and it never upsets me. I feel that they are doing *me* a favor in asking me to sign their program or something, and not the other way around. All I'm looking forward to is the day that John Travolta may ask me for my autograph so that I can get his in return.

Maybe I'm dwelling on something unimportant too long, but I think that even when you're tired of signing, especially after a tough round, it's something you owe your fans. If they are going to come out and spend money and tramp around to see me, then I can sign autographs. And every time you sign another one, you make a solid fan. People will really be on your side if you sign an autograph, or smile and say "hello." It's important to a golf fan, and golf fans are important to me.

But it sometimes just amazes me how people can react to me. They can make me very special, and frequently I think they're seeing someone else when they approach me— their daughter or something. That's not bad as long as they don't expect *too* much of me and remember that I'm young, and I'm human, and I can make mistakes. That's why I love the way my father is. He loves me emotionally as his daughter, but he has always treated me as a person.

I love the crew of "Nancy's Navy."

For that matter, I think most people are usually very considerate. No one has tried to rip my clothes off, or grab something of mine as a souvenir, or anything. The only gallery where I was a little scared was at a tournament held just outside New York City, but that was chiefly because the crowd was so big that they all pressed in on me, and I couldn't get from place to place. I had to have a kind of security protection there after the officials saw what was going on, but it all turned out to be okay in the end. Just more tiring than anywhere else I've been.

I got back to Roswell for the first time in almost two years later in 1978, to visit my Dad at home rather than only seeing him when he flew to see me on tour, and to give an exhibition and a clinic. It was really kind of nice to be back again, and I was touched by the way the people acted. I felt more than I ever have elsewhere that all these New Mexicans think of me as *their* Nancy Lopez. I make my home elsewhere now, because there are better places for a professional golfer to play out of and to practice in, but I'd hope that Roswell folk will always consider me their Nancy.

Now let's return to right after I won my fifth straight tournament and was being tabbed as Wonder Woman. What did Wonder Woman do next? She hit the skids for a few weeks, that's what she did.

She went out to try for win number six in a row in the Lady Keystone Open, held at the Hershey Country Club in Pennsylvania, and got snowed under! Or maybe buried under would be the better term. Pat Bradley shot a dandy 10-under-par 206 over a tough course to win, and my 5-over-par 221 got me no better than a tie for thirteenth place, far down the list. Sure I was a little disappointed that my streak had come to an end but not too much so, because a new streak that I hope will last me all my life began there in Hershey. You see, among the people who interviewed me was a television sportscaster from neighboring Harrisburg whose name was Tim Melton! And that's my name now, Nancy Lopez Melton! I wrote before that in golf you win some and lose some. In life it can be the other way around, and you can lose some and then win some!

It was nearing the end of the year and admittedly I was sort of pooped out, but so was everybody else, I guess. I did sustain a minor shoulder injury just then but that wasn't severe enough to be an alibi for the fact that in my next four tournaments, the final ones of the 1978 United States tour circuit, I finished anywhere from a tie for seventh to that Hershey tie for thirteenth—nothing better. The cry went up from those people unsophisticated about golf's ups

*One way to hit
the skids.*

Jane Blalock says "Don't be gone long!" as I pull out of the tour for a while with a sore shoulder

and downs, but who had seen me headlined for so many weeks, "What's happened to Nancy Lopez?" At that stage, if my golfing experience and savvy hadn't educated me philosophically to know the truth about "Win some, Lose some," I suppose I too might have wondered "What's happening to Nancy Lopez?" But that thought never crossed my mind. "I might be in something of a slump for a few weeks now," I felt, "but my winning number will be coming up soon enough again. That miracle of winning five in a row is probably a once-in-a-lifetime thing, and this is just a natural letdown. Play it cool. As a matter of fact I'm continuing to play well but for the time being others are playing better. Nicklaus's Law about 20 percent is simply gnawing away at my year's record to date. I'll show 'em after a little rest when I go overseas."

Well, that's the way it did work out, I'm happy to say. Along with almost all of the other leading women golfers, I went over to England in the fall to play in Europe's major women's event, the Colgate European Open, held at Sunningdale, and won it with three comfortable strokes to spare. It was a very prestigious and important title for me to capture and the perfect one in which to return to winning ways.

Then, in November, and once again accompanied by a substantial number of my most competitive rivals, I went to Japan for three events. In the first, the Mizuno Ladies' Classic, I finished in a three-way tie for first place with Michiko Okada of Japan and Ai-Yu Tu of Taiwan, and Michiko won over Ai-Yu and me on the fifth hole of a sudden-death play-off. Oh, well.

A few days later I played in that very interesting event at Kawasaki, which I mentioned earlier, the Rolex International Mixed Doubles Championship. That fine Mexican player, Ernesto Acosta, had not been accompanied by any

I was seven under par in winning the Ladies European Open

Mexican female partner, so Mexico had no entry. But as a Mexican American, I came pretty close to filling the bill and no one protested when it was suggested that we team up and compete for Mexico. Our fifty-four hole score won the event by three strokes over the next best finishers, the Japanese team, while the pair of Laura Baugh and Arnold Palmer took third place for the United States. It was a lovely, social affair as well as being a fascinating competitive one, the details of which I told you about in the chapter, about men's golf versus women's, and I enjoyed playing in it a lot, particularly since no one accused me of being another Benedict Arnold. I also enjoyed winning the women's individual title with my four-under-par 68 on one round.

But my most important Pacific victory came in the third and final golf meeting over there, the Far East Women's Invitation at Kuala Lumpur, in Malaysia. I shot a 216 for fifty-four holes over that tricky course and took the event by two strokes, which certainly closed out my year on a high note. I had won almost $200,000 in official prize money. In 1978 I won more prize money than any rookie ever had done before, male or female, and this despite the fact that men's purses are so very much bigger than ours: It was Jerry Pate's previous record that I broke. And between unofficial prize money and endorsements and other things that my business representatives fixed up for me (more of that later), I had earned a lot more than $200,000. Probably double that. I myself won't really know what the exact final figure is until someone, even better at mathematics than I am, prepares my income tax form, and that's still some time off from when this is being written. Besides, it is really only my own business and that of the IRS, isn't it?

So the reassuring conviction of "Win some, Lose Some" stood by me in that fabulous first year, when things did go a little sour for a short while, and even if my England and Far East tours hadn't turned out to be as super successful as they did, I'm mature enough now to have been philosophical about it. I know you can't win 'em all.

But I'll tell you something that, by this time, you may already suspect. I'm going to keep trying to do so, and I'll take some convincing before I truly believe it!

Chapter 7

That's the Way the Money Goes

My Education in Business Administration

IT CERTAINLY IS NO SECRET to us television watchers that all sports have become businesses. Whether you like it or not, it's a fact of life today that the bottom line carries the clout in most sports operations, and all sorts of business arise out of sports. There's Big Business, like multi-million dollar contracts for superstars. Show Business, like the way the Olympics and the Superbowl are staged. Even Funny Business, I'm afraid, like the use of drugs and "doping" and the occasional hints of a "fix" in boxing or horse racing.

Maybe I'm just an innocent or maybe I'm blind, but I've never seen any Funny Business at all in women's golf. The tour and all the people involved strike me as earnest and hard-working, and those who make money out of the game earn it by competence, devotion, and skill. So I'm not going to have a thing to say about Funny Business, but instead get down to the real business in professional golf, and what I've learned about it. First a little historical background would help, both about me and about the growth of the women's game.

When I was quite young, but already playing well, my

Dad built a trophy case in the den of our house in Roswell because it looked as if I was going to win a lot of trophies before I was done. And no matter how much pride we all might have in displaying them, they'd be so many dust catchers to add to Mom's housecleaning chores unless we got them stacked together somewhere neatly. Dad was an optimist about how I'd do, so he built the cabinet up from the floor right to the ceiling. For a while we had to fill in the empty spaces with dishes, but today there's an awful lot of silver crowding that trophy case, with one cup going all the way back to when I was eleven years old and was the youngest golfer ever to play in the Women's State Amateur. It's exciting for me when I go back home to look it all over and remember things. I still like trophies a lot, and there's always a bit of disappointment for me if I win a tournament and the prize money, even if it's big, is all you get. Then there's nothing to remember the event by. Still, there's no use kidding yourself about things, and maybe when my Dad looks at the case he remembers best how much money he had to spend to allow me to compete for those trophies. I really don't think so, but I do know that it was always his idea that some day I'd turn professional and it all would pay off, and I sure can't criticize that. I can only be thankful that it actually did work out that way. Nor can I deny that I had the same urge to earn money at golf, no matter how much I loved the silverware. In the last chapter of this book I'll be telling you more about how I feel today about the comparative rewards I get out of my golf.

Looking back even more years at the history of golf in this country, half a century ago professional golf was already big stuff for the men, but even then the standout was Bobby Jones, who remained an amateur all through his spectacular playing years. By the financial standards of those days, the money was good in pro golf, but it wasn't ever enough to attract Jones away from his distinguished career as a lawyer. And on the women's side, there just wasn't any professional golf at all. The female equivalents of Bobby Jones in those days were Joyce Wethered, of England, and Glenna Collett (later Glenna Collett Vare) of the United States and they competed only as amateurs. The amateur championships were *the* championships for the ladies.

It wasn't until the late 1940s that women's professional golf made any headway at all. Golfers like Patty Berg led the way, but even by 1948 there were only nine tournaments in all and the leading money winner, the great Babe Didrikson Zaharias, piled up a great big $3,400 in prize money. Still, at least it was a beginning and five years later, in 1953, when Louise Suggs topped the list, she had won about $20,000. That was a very decent sum to earn at that time, particularly for a woman, but of course no women golfers except the very best were in that money league— Zaharias and Suggs and Betsy Rawls and people like that.

By 1963 Mickey Wright had taken over as unquestionably the dominant player, and in that year there were twenty-eight tournaments and Mickey pulled down over $30,000 in official winnings. Now, in the late 1970s, there are thirty-six tournaments, which is not so very many more than back then, but in my rookie year of 1978 I won almost $200,000 officially, and there were three other women who topped $100,000 and another dozen or so who won more than $50,000 each. Over the years Kathy Whitworth has won almost a million dollars of official money and is still going strong. She started in 1959, became the leading money winner in 1965, and continued to be that every year for nine straight years except for 1969, when Carol Mann nosed her out by a thousand dollars. Kathy was third on the money list as recently as 1977, with over $100,000, and she won almost $70,000 in official money in 1978, but back in 1965 when she first took over as the tour leader she only won just under $30,000. The price of beef isn't the only thing influenced by inflation, but in the case of women's golf, it's been more than inflation. It's been the stimulus of business.

Money breeds money, and tournament official winnings are by no means everything a star makes these days. Big business comes sharply into the picture. As an example, my rookie year produced for me even more in appearances, commercial endorsements, and things like that, than the money I earned by doing well in tournaments.

We are plunged into the money game right from the outset of our professional lives, and heaven knows it's been awfully good for me. So even if I do still have a special love for trophies, and a sense of fellowship for what's called the amateur spirit, I sure wouldn't have wanted to have been born so early that I wouldn't have been able to cash in on my golf. No way. I'm a professional, and I'm both glad of it and proud of it.

The first time money raised its beautiful head with respect to my golf came, quite naturally, when I got feelers for a golf scholarship from a college. I wanted to get a scholarship for sure, because my Dad had worked and my Mom had sacrificed forever to keep things going for me to that point, and it was time for me to stand on my own two feet. In fact I told Dad flatly that I wasn't going to college at all unless I got a scholarship, and the college I wanted most was Arizona State, because I knew it had an exceptional golf team. My grades were good enough, and my golf was good enough, but what I didn't know was that Arizona State wasn't offering any golf scholarships at all to girls.

That was a big disappointment when I learned it, but then somebody told me that the University of Tulsa had more advanced feminist ideas, and that I ought to apply there. So I did, and Tulsa said they would take me and give me a half scholarship. That became my first solid experience in business negotiating. I said to them that I truly needed a full scholarship and that unless I got one I wasn't going to Tulsa.

I guess you can't actually hold your breath for two weeks, but it seems to me I did while I waited that length of time for the answer. But when it came it was "Yes," and the University of Tulsa seemed to have everything I needed or wanted. I heard that the educational program was good, and the university had all the money and people required to support the golf team in a big way. So I really was looking forward to going there, but during the summer before I was going to enter college I played in the U.S. Open championship, and even though it was my first time and I was still a young amateur, I came in second! As a result, I won the Colgate Golf Scholarship, which was a very big thing for me just then. It gave me a reason to reconsider, because it was a $10,000 four-year golf scholarship that would have allowed me almost to pick and choose among the colleges that featured a golf program, but I still decided in the end to stick with Tulsa. I had visited the school and had really liked everything I saw about it, from the fact that it was a fairly small private college, with a nice campus, to its being co-ed. It seemed to suit me just right.

So off I went to Tulsa, majoring at first in engineering as I've told you, and some of the subjects, like calculus, were really hard. Because I was on the golf team I was traveling a lot of the time, and that meant that I was missing classes that I desperately needed. You can't just read calculus or chemistry out of a book and get the idea very well. So although I did pass freshman year, I wasn't getting as good marks as I had in high school, and even though I changed to an easier major in sophomore year, I certainly wasn't on my way toward a Phi Beta Kappa key. Golf was taking up too much of my time to do a good scholastic job, and that's why I was really ready to stop college at the end of my second year and set out for a professional golfing life. You can't even begin to study the way a college student has to study if you're on the sort of athletic schedule we were. We went on a trip about one week in every three, and sometimes we'd go every second week. Florida and Texas and New Mexico and Oklahoma—we tried to play all over and in as many tournaments as we could because the money had been supplied to enable us to travel, and the college wanted us to make a showing. It would be good public relations for Tulsa—a good business investment. We did it right through the entire school year, so we never had a chance for a long stretch of no golf during which we might catch up on studies. So for me Tulsa was a sort of prep school for my real upcoming education, the subject of this book, becoming a woman golfer. And Tulsa gave me my second business experience after that first one of negotiating a full scholarship. Now as a member of its touring golf team, I had become an important member of the college's advertising department!

If all this sounds ungrateful of me, or conveys the idea that I didn't like Tulsa, I don't mean that at all. I really cared for the university and admired it. It's just that, as a golfer in a college where golf was important, I didn't get to learn much engineering or calculus or chemistry. I'll bet other nongolfers did.

Just before I turned professional I went off to qualifying school, and that was my introduction to the serious business side of golf. A man named Hughes Norton was there to talk to me. He is with International Management Group (IMG), a fabulous merchandising and financial management concern, based in Cleveland but with offices all over the world. It's headed up by a lawyer, Mark McCormack, who I think was the first one really to take a whole bunch of athletes under his wing and manage them financially so that they made a lot more money than if he weren't around. Sure, there had been managers of athletes before, but McCormack created a new sort of empire in the field that exposed and publicized his athletes to the hilt, got them commercial endorsements for products, handled and invested their earnings, and furnished legal and tax advice. It's a tremendous service for most of us, because professional athletes not only are not likely to be sophisticated about such matters but, even if they were, hardly have any time to give to them. So International Management does just about everything imaginable for its stable of athletes except play their sports for them and tell them when it's time to come in out of the rain. I think McCormack's first client, and certainly his biggest and best at the outset and probably ever since, was Arnold Palmer. McCormack himself is a good enough golfer to have played in the British Amateur, and he did so well for Palmer that his success, added to his being so high in golfing circles, attracted a flock of other golfers to IMG. Two of the very best joined up very soon, Jack Nicklaus and Gary Player, and although Nicklaus broke away later to form his own business organization, Palmer and Player are still with IMG, along with a number of other top-notch male golfers. They also represent a small number of women golfers such as Laura Baugh, Carol Mann, and Donna Young, and any time they feel someone is promotable, they have an eye out for him or her. Now that women's golf is expanding so fast, it's a sure bet that more of us will be linking up with McCormack or some outfit like his. I know IMG has done wonders for me.

Looking over the Palm Coast layout with Arnold Palmer

Golfers aren't the only athletes that International Management handles by a long shot. Business is business, and there's a lot of it in other sports too, so just as a partial list, in tennis they manage the affairs of Björn Borg, Vitas Gerulaitis, Evonne Goolagong, Virginia Wade, Billie Jean King, Rod Laver, and John Newcombe. In boxing, Muhammad Ali is their client. In skiing, Jean-Claude Killy. In car racing, Jackie Stewart. They even have something to do with Dennis the Menace!

Soon after I'd met Hughes Norton, he traveled out to Roswell to discuss things more with my parents and me, and he sold us the idea of my hitching up with International Management right after I turned professional. I've never regretted it. They've taken a million details off my hands and have more than doubled the money winnings I made on the tour. And there's one thing they *don't* do that I appreciate a lot. Although they're naturally eager to get me sponsors, they never let me in for endorsing something I don't like, or that they think doesn't fit the image that they feel is my best appeal. Since I suppose that image has some basis in fact, that I'm the golfer who might be that nice, wholesome girl next door, I'm happy to go along with it. I certainly not only don't want to be built up as a swinger or a sex symbol, but that's not my style anyhow. So IMG has turned down quite a lot of commercial offers from companies selling things like feminine hygiene, or revealing clothes designed for a seductive, slinky type. But there's no denying that appearance has a lot to do with pleasing our sponsors and keeping them happy with us, as well as pleasing ourselves, and we women golfers are very conscious of it and work at it. More of that a little later.

IMG has signed me up to endorse a number of things that do suit me, and which I actually like and use. One is a golf practice device called Power Swing, which you might look at and wonder what's so good about it, but which really does a job. I can practice on it for a while and then, when I walk out to the first tee to play a round, I feel as if I'd whacked out dozens of balls and am in the groove. I'm all warmed up and everything, and besides I've found out it's great for your muscle and body tone.

I have a contract with the Florida Citrus Commission to promote orange juice, and have turned out a TV commercial for them. That's absolutely an honest endorsement because I love the stuff and drink it all the time. You can't get more girl-next-doory than orange juice, can you? And you can say much the same for another product I've plugged on television, Rose Milk, the skin care cream, but I did that for Japan's TV network.

Of course a really big tie-in for me is with the whole Colgate line. They're the people who started me out with that golf scholarship, and Colgate is the chief sponsor for women's professional golf overall. I play with Ram golf clubs, which are owned by Colgate, and there is even a line of Nancy Lopez golf clubs in the works. A lot of us women golfers favor Ram clubs, and quite a few of the best men too, like Tom Watson, Gary Player, and Ray Floyd. I also did a commercial for Colgate toothpaste, which I always used long before my affiliation with the Colgate-Palmolive people. So that's a very solid and gratifying connection.

Then I represent Palm Coast, a development of Florida's east coast—the Gold Coast—near Daytona Beach. I am the touring pro of the development and I like the area so much that I bought a condominium there, where I hope to spend a lot of time in the future. As for other things, I'm involved with Sun Life of Canada, and I've already written about Fila, the Italian apparel manufacturer, and there are a number of other arrangements that International Management produced for me, like getting me on the *Johnny Carson*, and *Good Morning America*, and the *Dinah Shore*, and the *Today* shows, plus an arrangement to be a contributor to *Golf Digest* magazine, and the contract for this book, but those are the main ones up to now. It's kept me sort of busy dealing with all those business matters. Hughes Norton is the man who talked me into going with International, but Peter Johnson is the one who's taken care of me and my affairs ever since. He seems to be my agent, manager, financial adviser, guardian, and friend all rolled into one, and if there's anything he doesn't happen to know about, there's always someone at IMG who does and Peter passes it along to me.

Once I start making money from any source, tournament winnings or outside things that IMG sets up for me, it all goes directly to them and they deposit it between a savings account and a checking account in my name until I have a chance to come to Cleveland and talk with them about investing some of it. I now own some stocks and one bond, and I put some money into a gas well speculation that they recommended and, Bingo!, they hit gas! So I've a regular income coming in from that too. Then they've put some of my earnings into a retirement plan, the Keogh plan, which theoretically pays off some terrific sum at age sixty-five if I make it that far, but I'm actually more interested at the moment in something they're working on now. It's a plan for all their athletes to be able to get a secure and decent retirement series of payments at a much earlier age, and that's interesting because it's a long stretch between when a pro athlete is too old to be any good, and age sixty-five!

IMG never really dictates matters and I appreciate that. They simply advise me and I make my own decisions after calling my Dad and talking it over with him. You know he was a 3-handicap golfer, and that's about what I think he'd be rated as a financial advisor too, because without making so very much money he has always done pretty well building up what he has made, and my guess is that his advice is just about as good as anybody's.

All of this really kept me jumping that first year. Between traveling to tournaments, playing in them, honoring the commitments I had made for appearances and exhibitions, no day was long enough. I wore myself out because quite honestly everything was fun and irresistible—it was like being Cinderella at the ball. But I paid a price in never being able to get in the practice I wanted and needed, and I finally reached the stage where I was literally pooped physically. After my seventh victory of the year, which was the same tournament as my fifth in a row, I really tailed off, at least in this country, for the balance of the season. Up to then nobody but me had won more than one tournament, and great performers like Donna Young and Kathy Whitworth and Judy Rankin hadn't won any at all.

But Kathy and Judy each did win a tournament before the year ended, and Donna won two during those couple of months when I wasn't making headlines. Hollis Stacy took the big one, the U.S. Open, and Janie Blalock and Pat Bradley continued to have good years, but at the end after I'd recovered my strength and went abroad and won the Colgate European and the Far East Open, the final statistics for the year looked like this:

	TOUR EVENTS	FINISHES 1st	2nd	3rd	SCORING AVERAGE
Nancy Lopez	25	9	2	0	71.76
Jane Blalock	26	4	4	1	71.98
Pat Bradley	29	3	2	4	72.31

No on else won more than two events or had a scoring average lower than 72 strokes per round, so I have to be pretty satisfied with my first year on the tour. My 275 (13 under par) in the LPGA Championship was the year's lowest score, I won the Vare Trophy for lowest scoring average, and I was named both golf's Rookie of the Year and its Golfer of the Year, and the Associated Press voted me Female Athlete of the Year.

All of this has been very good for business, of course, and I'm now in a solid enough financial position to be able to catch my breath and be more selective about what I do. I still want to play in all major golf tournaments and a great many of the others, but if I want to say "No thanks" now and then to a nice, juicy fee offered to me to play in an exhibition match, I can afford to do so. International Management is a big corporation but it has a big enough heart to go with it to understand that a girl needs some hours off to sleep, listen to records, wash her hair, watch television, and even spend some time with her husband.

LPGA Commissioner Ray Volpe presents the Vare Trophy

You can see that a lot of meaningful golf business really gets pumped up by Show Business. Without national exposure to the public, and that means television coverage and commercials to a large extent, athletes could never continue to take in the money they do. Now, and really for the first time, women's golf is becoming a popular television attraction, just as men's has been for some time. It's quite wonderful how the television cameras cover all the big moments in a golf tournament, shifting all the time from player to player, off the tee, following the flight of the ball, zooming in on the putting green, and always catching a critical moment as it occurs or, if two such things are going on at the same moment, running the one they missed a minute later on replay. It's absolute magic how they do it, and the people who care about promoting golf are very much in television's debt. As a result, television has been a big factor in turning practically all major golf events into medal play affairs, where once quite a few were match play. It's something of a shame that at our level match play has almost disappeared, because it's the original basic game of golf and the way most amateur weekend players compete against each other. Also it's fun sometimes to battle one person head-to-head, rather than always simply trying to play your best, mechanically perfect golf, to try to score in low figures. However there are severe drawbacks for the television industry in trying to cover a match play tournament.

The first and most obvious one is that the biggest stars, who naturally draw the most interest, may well be eliminated in an early round. Lose to someone once in a match play event and you're out, of course. In men's golf (not to be personal), for instance, let's imagine a match play tournament with a draw sheet of sixty-four top-notch golfers, the most successful and charismatic of whom, at the moment, might be Jack Nicklaus, Tom Watson, Gary Player, and Lee Trevino. Ideally, from the television standpoint, these four will reach the semifinals, guaranteeing two drawing-card matches on the next to last day and one irresistibly attractive final on the last day. That would certainly pull the best Nielsen rating by far. However it's almost sure that things won't work out that way, and that at least one or two of those players, and perhaps all four, will be bumped off somewhere along the first four rounds that have to be played to reduce a field of sixty-four down to the four semifinalists. Staying with our imagination (and once again nothing personal intended), let's suppose that such great golfers as Lou Graham, Craig Stadler, Bruce Lietzke, and Bill Kratzert become the semifinalists. That's more than quite possible. All of them were among the leading money winners last year, and each is completely capable of beating anyone in the world on a given day. But their names are not so well known to the general public, so a lot of television viewers, who don't appreciate that the golf may be just as good and interesting as if Nicklaus were playing Watson, will flick their dials to a channel that's showing an old Marx Brothers comedy. Down go the Nielsen ratings for golf.

In a medal play event, on the other hand, the person or persons in whom the viewer is most interested may be well off the lead, and really have virtually no chance to win, but at least he or she is still playing and will be shown now and then making a brilliant shot. And perhaps a miracle will take place, as surprisingly often does happen, and your favorite will be back in there up front with the other leaders. So the set stays tuned to the channel showing golf.

The second drawback to televising a match play tournament is that so many matches don't last right up to the eighteenth hole. If a player is five holes up with only four to play, the match is over after the fourteenth hole. So having the television cameras merely covering the final four holes, as is so often done because it's economical and all the final drama in a medal play tournament takes place there, just won't do for a match play tournament.

To be sure of catching the end of a match the TV people have to cover every hole from the tenth through the eighteenth, which is a lot more work and a lot more expensive. In addition, if enough matches do conclude early before the eighteenth green, the entire late afternoon's schedule will be fouled up with no more golf to show and the better part of an hour's programming left unfilled. The station may be reduced to showing a couple of Three Stooges shorts.

The result of the very understandable preference of television to cover medal play only is probably why we women have only one match play tournament. That is the Colgate Triple Crown, with the sixteen players who have qualified by doing best in the previous year's Colgate tournaments competing individually one against the other, as in a tennis draw, until the eventual winner emerges in the final. That tournament is televised despite the possible drawbacks because it's the first major event of the year, even though the prize money isn't part of "official winnings," and it's an interesting event for most viewers simply because it's different and they don't see this type of play very often. But from a business standpoint, it does present the problems connected with television that I just explained, and if the popular favorites fall by the wayside in an early round, it's also likely to cut down the size of the actual gallery that comes out to the course to watch during the last couple of rounds over the weekend. Instead of the many thousands we often draw each day over a tournament, maybe many fewer will show up. That's not only bad for the gate receipts but it doesn't make the tournament look so important on television.

So Show Business has to be a major consideration for all of us, if we're to benefit the most from Big Business and, as I hinted earlier in Chapter 3, looking attractive is part of it. But it isn't enough just to dress nicely. You want to do that, of course, but you've got to work on your own physical appearance and well-being, particularly if you don't start out being Laura Baugh or Jan Stephenson. It's good for your own ego and health. It's good for your golf game. And your sponsors know it's very good for them.

Women golfers, therefore, certainly do care about the way they look on the course and on television. A lot of us were naturally heavy, for example, and we've lost an amazing amount of weight as a group. The LPGA keeps statistics on that, and simply on that basis our image must have improved a lot right across the field. In my own case, I've always had to watch my weight. Even though I was a really skinny young girl, I was up to 165 pounds when I went to college and that's a lot of poundage for a 5′4½-inch girl. I didn't look as good as I knew I could and I wasn't playing golf as well as I had just before college. My whole timing was off. You know, excess weight affects your shoulder turn and the entire pivot of the swing. But as soon as I lost some weight my swing and my timing came back and, what is more, I didn't get nearly as tired when I was playing. I felt real good, both on the course and when I took a look in a mirror.

So ever since then I am careful about what I eat. I have a good breakfast because I believe in that, but I settle for a salad at lunch. For dinner I'll usually have fish or chicken and vegetables, but no potatoes. I hardly every eat bread when I'm on a good fitness program, and I take vitamin and mineral supplements. Ideally I think 130 pounds would be my best weight, but I have to admit that I'm usually 10 or 15 pounds over that. I could get down lower, because dieting isn't too hard for me, but I'm always afraid that if I lose too much weight I may lose too much distance on my shots too, and distance is a big factor in giving me an edge against most women players. So I have to strike a balance between what's best for my golf and what might be better for my looks, and that's what I try to do. In any case, I get out of as many planned dinners and banquets as I can, because they don't serve salads and cottage cheese as the main course at most of those. When I do go, I'm careful, and just sort of poke my food around with my fork and take an occasional bite. One thing that helps at those affairs is that I don't drink at all.

Nor do I smoke. Both my mother and father were smokers when I was a little girl, but Dad quit fifteen years ago and Mom did too a few years later. In her case I saw what smoking did to her. She suffered terrible chest pains, and only got relief when she stopped smoking, so I made up my mind then and there that I'd never pick up the habit. And although I grew up in school at a time when a lot of kids were into marijuana and other things, I never was even tempted. I was always having a good time anyway and I didn't feel I needed anything like that. Besides, even the idea that I might lose control of myself panicked me then and still would. I think the women on the tour feel the same way. You read about the use of drugs in sports but I personally have never seen people in our group who ever took anything more than something like aspirin.

As for exercise, of course I play a lot of golf, and that involves miles of walking. The actual swinging of a golf club isn't much exercise, even if you're a bad golfer and have to take a lot of strokes per round, but walking is good. In addition I do some stretching exercises including something like fifty sit-ups a day, and that's about it. I visit a health spa to use a Nautilus weight machine as often as every other day whenever I'm near one, which is usually.

That tones up my body wonderfully, I feel, but I think doing it every day is too much. I'd rather give my muscles an in-between day to repair themselves naturally before I tackle them again with a Nautilus workout.

Let's go back to thinking about the business end of golf again, and what's likely to be in store for the very fine young woman golfer who may not reach the heights, even if she takes care of herself and plays very well. There are well over a hundred of us on the LPGA roster and last year the official winnings ranged from my close to $200,000 down through the great many I've told you about who made really big money, with all of us profiting even more because of commercial extras. But the less successful you are, obviously the fewer of those extras are offered you, and many of the women don't earn more than perhaps $10,000 or $15,000 a year in winnings, and that's it. How do they make out compared, let's say, to an office worker who makes that sort of salary?

Well, a lot of the girls come thinking that the tour sounds awfully glamorous and that you live luxuriously while just playing golf. And you have your picture taken a lot, and appear on TV, and you get a great big golf bag with your name painted on it. Well, it's not all that by a long shot, and certainly not at the beginning unless you start winning big right away. I think that probably the average costs for anybody to do everything comfortably, flight and car transportation, and accommodations, and food, and paying the caddy and all that, is not far from $1,000 a week. Clearly $10,000 or $15,000 a year won't even begin to cover expenses at that standard, even over a thirty-week season, and you do have to live the rest of the year too, when you're not earning money at golf. So what's the answer? Either your parents or someone furnishes extra support, or you go into the hole with your manager if you have one, or maybe you give up. The partial answer for many girls is to cut down expenses as far as they can, but then that dream of a luxurious life goes out the window. They team up as roommates and bunk down in a cheaper motel, and they grab a hamburger or something at a McDonalds or Wendy's for dinner. They ride buses. It isn't easy and the LPGA understandably, for the good of our organization, has rules that may make it even harder. Because some of the girls come on the tour just to be able to say that they're professionals and are on it, but if they don't produce they can't last. First of all, you can't just sign up. You have to qualify, and that's a strict test. Then first-year players have to compete in a certain minimum number of tournaments and win a minimum amount of money to stay on the roster the next year. Second-year players have comparable sorts of requirements that are somewhat more severe, although quite attainable if you're serious. But you can't just come out and play a few times and be on the LPGA tour very long. They don't want the tournaments cluttered up with noncontenders, and they always have to clear some part of the deck for newcomers each year. It makes sense.

The LPGA is a great organization that runs our world for our joint benefit. I really can't think of anything significant to criticize about it, even if I think sometimes that they're awfully strict about comparatively unimportant rules. But golf depends upon its rules as far as play is concerned, and rules are honored so much in our game that probably it's wise that administrative rules get carried out equally without favor or argument. For instance, you can't play in another tournament while an LPGA tournament is going on, although you're allowed one exemption from that rule per year if you ask for it. I ran up against a problem toward the end of last year in connection with that rule. I had already been granted my one exemption and had taken it, but after my dry spell in July and after I had found my game again and won the Colgate European in August, I was keen to go to Japan and play in the tournaments there. But I'd be missing an official LPGA tournament in Dallas if I did that. So I called our commissioner, Ray Volpe, and asked for an extra exemption and I didn't get it before I had to leave, so the LPGA fined me. Fair enough, I suppose, and I even may have been a factor in the LPGA's changing the rule this year to allow two exemptions, which seems to be a sensible relaxing of a possibly too severe rule.

Then there was the time last year when Patty Berg, who was sixty years old, wanted to team up with Gene Sarazen, who was well into his seventies, and play in a mixed team event with us. But they said that they would only do so if they were permitted to use a golf cart, because both felt it would not be sensible to walk the entire tournament distance. Sarazen hadn't done anything like that in years. Well, this tournament is run by the LPGA and by the PGA in alternate years and the PGA happened to be in charge at the time. The rules committee decided that Patty and Gene couldn't use a cart and I'll grant that technically they were absolutely right. After all, if you ever bend the rules even a little bit you open the way to the dam bursting, but Patty Berg's and Gene Sarazen's appearance in one of our tournaments, and one that was more of a social affair than anything important, would have been very nice. She is one of the greatest women players of all time and he one of the men's, and just to see them out there together would have been heartwarming to a lot of people. (Just to complete the story, Patty Berg did indeed play thirty-six holes, with a young partner, as an added attraction to the event, and she walked all the way.)

So maybe I'm wrong, but I do wonder if allowing her and Sarazen to use a cart would have been so sacrilegious as to

Patty Berg still going strong today

overthrow the traditions of the Royal and Ancient Golf Club at St. Andrews, where the rules were born?

But don't get me wrong. I'm a great admirer of all the people who administer golf, especially our strict LPGA commissioner, Ray Volpe, and Betsy Rawls, and the public relations chief, Chip Campbell, and I couldn't wish for any group that's more dedicated to us and to golf. Everything they do is with the good of the game in mind, and everybody who works for a living would be lucky to have bosses as fair as the LPGA. As far as my fine and the Patty Berg decision are concerned, employees like me always have their little gripes, you know.

Chapter 8

A Mixed Threesome

My Education in Chemistry

YOU CLICK WITH CERTAIN PEOPLE and they with you. Good vibes bounce back and forth between you and sometimes there's no explaining it, because you can be two very different sorts of people and still it happens. It must be chemistry.

I'd like to tell you something about two very important people like that, for me. Of course, standing all alone and not to be lumped with anyone is Tim, and our story clearly is the one I'm itching to get to, but first I'm going to write about my caddie, Roscoe Jones, not only because he's so valuable a sidekick in my golf game but because he figures in the Nancy-Tim story, as you'll learn a little later.

Caddies, at least on the women's tour, which is all I know about, are quite different than what I understand they once were. They used to be anything from kids to older men who were out there to earn a few dollars a day by lugging clubs around the course and looking for lost balls. The exceptions were talented poor youngsters who had golfing ambitions themselves, who studied good players while they were caddying, and who later became a Gene Sarazen, a Walter Hagen, a Lee Elder, or a Lee Trevino.

Today the caddies are more likely to be rather well educated men who will eventually have something more than caddying to do, but meanwhile who find it a pleasant and often even a profitable thing to do. A few are already in business or a profession, but caddying and becoming a part of the circuit intrigues them, almost the way an interesting summer job does a college student. They can pick up pleasant spending money and travel a lot while doing it, and a few, like Roscoe, do considerably better than that. I pay Roscoe a flat fee per week, win or lose, and it wouldn't be an ungenerous amount even if he didn't get anything else. But if I have a good year, like my rookie season, Roscoe makes out very well, because I cut him in for 10 percent of my winnings when I win a tournament. You can figure out how that makes a nice series of bonuses.

When I first came out on the tour, a young lawyer named Bruce Lamdon was caddying for my friend, Jo Ann Washam. We liked each other and he took me out for dinner a few times, and he talked to me about the tour. The people on it, and who might be good friends and be helpful to me, and stuff like that. He himself became my best friend at that time, so when he asked me if I was looking for a really good professional caddy, because he knew of one, I listened. That was how I hooked up with Roscoe, who had been about to quit the tour. We tried each other out in a tournament on Long Island where I finished second, and I was convinced that Roscoe not only knew his job but, even more important perhaps, had the right personality to help my game. He got the yardage down precisely, and he also was a very positive person who didn't raise any doubts or negative ideas in my mind. I've always had confidence, but Roscoe kind of gave me double confidence. Chemistry.

In practice sessions, we work as a team. I'll take a club, maybe an 8-iron, hit a few shots with it, and then we'll pace it off to see if I'm hitting it that day the distance we both know I should. Roscoe has got his pace down so pat that you could use it as a yardstick, which is just what we do. So when I'm playing a hole, and he's marked our card with some notation that indicates that the spot where my ball is lying is 150 yards from the green, I *know* that my 7-iron will be just right. I don't want to know anything else, and Roscoe doesn't try to tell me anything else. (He did once try something, and I'll tell you about it, but never again and not any more.) I want my caddy to back me up in my positive attitude when going after a shot, and it's the biggest reason in my mind why Roscoe is a good caddy. Anybody can carry clubs around.

Let me give you an example of the other side of the coin

On the tee with JoAnn Washam

—what I *don't* want in a caddie. I've had caddies who did a good job of pacing the yardage on a course before a tournament, jotting down various things along the way that can act as markers and tell us the distance from there to the green. This tree might be 180 yards away on one hole, that water fountain 135 yards away on another, and so forth. If you pinpoint at least a couple of locations like that for each hole, it makes proper club selection much easier when the times comes.

But the bad caddies (for me) about whom I'm writing, have been likely to answer something like this, when I've asked them the yardage for a shot coming up. "It's 165 yards and there's a trap on the far side of the green." *Darn it!* I don't want to *know* about that trap! I want to know the yardage and concentrate upon hitting the right shot for that yardage, and that's all I want to know! Being made aware of a danger that may lie in wait if I make a mistake, and hit the ball too far, is nothing but the planting of negative thinking in my mind. I want to fix my attention 100 percent on executing the shot at hand, with no nagging distraction. If I do goof and wind up in that trap, that will be the time I'll turn 100 percent of my attention to the next shot I'll be taking out of it, but right now I don't want to know that trap even exists.

Roscoe understands that, agrees with it, and he'd never be guilty of being negative with me. He bucks me up and tells me I *can* hit any shot, and that's what I value about him as a caddie. But over and above that, he understands how I feel about a lot of things and he tries to take care of me in many ways, like shooing away and screening me from unwelcome attention. I've told you that I'm likely to be something of a loner on the tour, and the result has been that Roscoe has really become my closest friend while the tour is going on. We travel together from place to place

We did it, Roscoe!

and have fun and often eat together, but I did actually
almost fire him once. He wasn't being negative about my
golf, but he got so possessive about me that he started to be
too positive! He got to the point during a round where he'd
tell me where or how to hit the ball, suggesting I lay up, or
hit a little fade shot, or take more sand in a bunker, and
things like that. If I wanted that sort of advice (and by this
time you know that, right or wrong, I don't!) I'd know wiser
places to go for it than Roscoe who, regardless of his many
other virtues, isn't much of a golfer.

When I didn't do the things Roscoe said, he not only got
mad but he showed it in his manner. Then I got mad myself, and we had a big fight about it at the Women's International, at Hilton Head. I told him he was putting too

much pressure on me, and that when the tournament was over, I didn't want him to caddy for me anymore.

That night Roscoe came to see me and admitted that perhaps I was right, and how about giving him another try? I answered that I didn't know, because I had already sounded out another caddie for the following week, so why didn't we each hook up with someone else, at least for that one week, and see how it worked out? Roscoe said that if he wasn't going to caddy for me, he didn't want to caddy for anybody. I couldn't resist that sort of loyalty, so we shook hands and went off together the next week to the Greater Baltimore Classic, which I won by three strokes over Donna Young. And that was the beginning of my five-wins-in-a-row streak! Roscoe and I must have solved our problem.

We're a good team. We don't walk the fairways together too much of the time, since he's usually checking yardage while I'm heading right toward the spot where my ball is, and also I walk faster than he does. But we talk between shots whenever it's easy and practical, and I find it a helpful way to relax then. If you just babble away about anything at all, it helps you regroup and focus your concentration when you need it for the next shot.

Anyway, Roscoe's been my caddie ever since, except on my trips abroad. In England, they don't allow you to have your own personal caddie, but simply assign one to each golfer for the tournament. I've had the same one, a man named Peter Coleman, for both of the past two years. Peter is a lot older than Roscoe, who's only five years older than me, but he's a very good caddie and we get along well. When I won in England with Peter doing my caddying, I hear that Roscoe took a lot of kidding. His pals said it looked as if Nancy didn't need him at all, and when I came back Roscoe shook his finger at me and said not to ever do

Peter Coleman picks out the right club in England

that again! If he wasn't caddying, don't win! Of course, he was kidding, but I do think it bothered him a little, and I guess I didn't help matters when I went off a short while later and won in Japan with a woman caddie! But Roscoe seems to have forgiven me.

The caddies in Japan invariably seem to be women. They all wear big, brimmed hats and very long-sleeved blouses as they pull your bag along in a cart behind you. They are absolutely dedicated to your success, and know their business thoroughly. It's tough to converse with them unless you know Japanese, so even though they're smart about yardage, and how far you can hit a ball with each club, there's no way to really discuss matters with them. You look over the shot and select what seems the right club, and then cock an inquiring eyebrow at your caddie. She either beams and nods "Yes," or shakes her head and picks out another club. You accept that or you don't, but on the whole I found it was a pretty good idea to go along with their judgment, because they really know the courses. But I still prefer Roscoe by some miles.

During my streak of five straight victories, Roscoe got interviewed almost as much as me. I was on the cover of eight major magazines, but each inside story included its part about Roscoe including one whose actual title was "A Caddie Named Roscoe." So when we got to Hershey, Pennsylvania, a few days before the tournament in which I was going to try for number six in a row, there was a television sportscaster from WHP-TV in nearby Harrisburg, all ready to cut tapes with both of us. His name was Tim Melton.

Tim tells the television station he won't be back this afternoon

Talk about chemistry! The tapes became very incidental as he interviewed me, and I kept thinking about him long after the session was over. Then, in the couple of days preceding the tournament, I kept running into him when I was out practicing on the course. I became very shy and not knowing quite how to act each time I saw or talked to him, and that wasn't at all like me. I'm not even a bit shy normally, and I never blush or get embarrassed, but I felt that way whenever I ran into Tim. So I confided to Roscoe that I thought that TV guy from Harrisburg was real cute, and I hadn't even caught his name when he introduced himself. Roscoe said why don't you go out with him, and I said well, I don't usually go up and ask a gentleman out, and Roscoe said to leave it up to him! I protested, "No, No!" If he wanted to take me out, he'd ask me.

It turned out this way. After seeing me shoot a 73 in the first round, while Pat Bradley, the eventual winner, was posting a 70 and Jane Blalock, who finished second, a 67, Tim asked Roscoe to come over to a corner of the press tent and tell him why I wasn't playing as well at Hershey as I had been. You know, Hershey's where my streak did end, and it might not have mattered how well I played because Pat wiped us all out, following her 70 with a 69 and then a 67. But I never was close, and the reason was that I was dead tired by then. From a golfing and health standpoint I probably should have skipped that particular tournament altogether but, as it turned out, I'm awfully glad I didn't. Because Roscoe replied to Tim that he might do better asking me that question himself, and that if he were to ask me out to dinner, he thought I'd go.

Tim later told me that he didn't really believe Roscoe because, as a general rule, he'd found you can't trust what caddies tell you, but he decided to risk it. Meanwhile Roscoe tipped me off about what he'd done, so I was prepared and when Tim actually did ask me for a date I said, "Sure! Sure!" probably before he had gotten the full invitation out. I was so excited that it had happened. The chemistry was really acting up!

We ate that first time in an Italian restaurant in town, and we got along so well that Tim took me out as often as possible all the rest of the week and for the extra two days I stayed over at the hotel on the Hershey golf course, after the tournament. For my part, I just knew that there was something about us two, and with Tim's job and home being in Harrisburg, he had to drive something close to an hour in each direction every day to take me out. So his chemistry must have been acting up too! It was weird. I stayed on those two days even though I should have been on my way to the Mayflower tournament in Indiana, but I had to know if something real was in the wings.

Tim has told me he thought that surely, as soon as I left, the chances were that I'd forget him, but the fact is that when I did leave, each of us would take turns calling the other on the phone to talk and say how much we missed each other. Tim solved that by flying out to Columbus a couple of weeks later to watch me play in the event there, and then he asked me to go back with him to Harrisburg and meet his parents. That kind of shocked me, because it was so fast, but it was a nice shock. The Meltons live in Medford Lakes, New Jersey, and we all liked each other, so the chemistry continued to be good.

I called Tim "cute" before, and maybe it's a strange word for a twenty-nine year-old guy who's about 6 feet 3 inches and weighs 215 pounds, but I think he's cute. You might prefer "handsome," or "macho," and that last is a good word for me to use because of my Mexican-American background. Anyway, I like the word and it fits Tim. He's big and strong-looking and very masculine, and I like all those things. Maybe, because I'm real feminine in my tastes, they add up for me, at least, to being cute!

We met in late June, and Tim asked me to marry him not very long after that and I said "Yes." But the very next day he seemed to have become a little jumpy about committing himself, because he said he'd been thinking about it all night, and maybe we ought to wait a little bit more so that we'd both be absolutely sure we weren't rushing into marriage. I had to go off for a week to a tournament, and while a week isn't very long, it seemed awfully long to me. But Tim telephoned toward the end of it and said that he was miserable, and that he was missing me incredibly, and now he was sure he couldn't get along without me and yes! —let's make it certain and definite right now! I guess I made it even more certain and definite a very short time later. The *Today* show had me on, and I blurted it out (secretly) to the fifty million people or so who watch *Today* every morning! I never claimed to be shy!

But you know, that wasn't the first time that Tim showed himself more cautious than I. In Harrisburg, when I was visiting his parents, and before he ever proposed to me, he took me to a baseball game. The program notes said that one certain player was single whereas, about another player, he was described as being a bachelor. I looked up at Tim and asked innocently what was the difference? Tim said that "single" meant someone who planned to get married in the future, or at least hoped to, while a "bachelor" was someone who never would. Well, I asked him, which are you? He said "bachelor," and I didn't see any grin as he said it, and it made me *so* mad! Because I knew I was falling in love with him, and his saying that just sort of popped my bubble, I guess. I was mad the rest of the night, but then later, when we did decide to get married, Tim asked me if I remembered that day at the ball game, and what he said.

I replied that I sure did. He said, "I knew what answer you were looking for and I did the opposite just to see how you'd react and for fun. I remember you were mad at me all the way through the game and afterwards, but it was just a lover's tease."

We were going to get married in the fall of 1979, and then we moved the date forward to April, but once he had taken the plunge Tim was all for not putting it off that long. So we finally picked an even earlier date, January 6, which was my twenty-second birthday, and sent out the invitations. About a hundred and fifty people attended, which was just about everybody we asked who was able to make it through the snow and the sleet and the freezing rain that fell alternately that day. Of course my Dad and Delma and

Bernie Guevara, Jr. may be my most enthusiastic fan

Bernie Guevara were there, along with my niece, Dana, and my nephew, Bernie, Jr. Bernie, Jr. was persuaded to have the good taste not to wear his T-shirt that says "Aunt Nancy Number 1" to the wedding. Tim's sister and nephew and niece were there too. One of the nicest guests to see there came all the way down from Rochester and, considering the weather conditions that understandably stopped some people, we appreciated his making the effort. That was Dr. Jerry Mesolella, the dentist I had bopped on the head with a drive that went astray during the Bankers Trust Classic back in June.

The Cathedral in the Woods, at Medford Lakes, is a lovely log cabin church, set among pine trees, and it looked

Snow and all, we got us to the church on time!

particularly pretty in all that snow and ice which, for once, made me perfectly glad to be sitting in the rear seat of the car and letting someone else drive. Anyway, I wasn't really dressed for the occasion—driving I mean. I was wearing a really lovely but quite elaborate wedding dress with all the trimmings. Veil and a long train and all that. After the reception we went to Philadelphia and spent the night in a hotel there, and the following morning took off on our honeymoon. I have to say that Hawaii's weather didn't live up to its reputation that week. It was cloudy almost all the time and raining a good part of it, but Tim and I didn't really care. It's such a beautiful place just to be in that we were not very golf-minded. We did potch around for six holes one time and Tim shot a par on one hole, where I took a bogey. So that made his day because Tim isn't quite as good on the golf course as he is at everything off it.

The previous year I had not really felt that I was mature enough to get married, even though my school boyfriend, Ron Benedetti, and I did become engaged for a while. But we had always known that we were going to wait at least two years, and I'm not sure either of us was convinced marriage would ever really happen. We were not only very young but we were realistic enough to know that I'd be traveling almost all the time during that frantic first year on the tour, and that I was going to want to go out with other people. I was always truthful with Ron and told him how I felt, and he was completely understanding. He told me I had to live and act the way I thought right for me, and when we eventually broke off our engagement, perhaps it was something of a relief for both of us.

But with Tim, you may wonder if the same problem exists. It doesn't for a couple of reasons. First, before I was married, I used to love being alone in a hotel room on the tour, where I didn't even have to make my bed let alone ever cook anything or clean up. Now I feel lonely out there, and am eager to get back to Tim and our own place. So I'm being more selective about how many and which tournaments I play in, and I can afford to do that now from the financial angle. Tim and I are keeping an apartment in Hershey as long as Tim's job in Harrisburg requires him to be in that area, but he hopes to expand his TV work elsewhere and we both agree that, in the long run, it's his career that is likely to decide where we eventually live. Right now we also have the condominium at Palm Coast, Florida, the development with which I have a commercial affiliation, and we'll spend as much time there as we can. And in the short run—the next five or ten years—once again we're both agreed that my golf and its demands are going to have to come first, because now is the time I can continue to make hay while the sun is shining, so to speak. Some day, not too many years off, I want to settle down and have children, but right now . . .

I still want to be the best golfer out there!

Tim knows that and he has no intention of even slowing me up, let alone stopping me. It's such a big sacrifice for him that it's the main reason why I felt I ought to make a big sacrifice of my own if he wanted it, and he did. The Meitons are very staunch Southern Baptists, and Tim wanted to be married in his church. We Lopezes, of course, are Catholics and I have always loved the Catholic religion. I even loved it when my mother used to sit me down and time me when she set me a prayer to learn. She'd say, "I want you to know this and I'll come back to hear you in ten minutes!" So converting from being a Catholic to becoming a Baptist was a tough decision for me, but it would have been every bit as hard, and probably even more so, for Tim to go the other way. We both felt that it was important for two married people, who are both religious, to share the same religion, and now that I've studied the Baptist faith a little, I feel that the basic beliefs are close enough that I'll grow to love the Baptist service just as I did the Catholic, even though they're a little different. On the tour there's play on Sundays and you don't have time to go to church, so they have FCA meetings on Tuesday nights—the Fellowship of Christian Athletes—and I've seen that people of different branches of Christianity can worship God together. That's how I came to feel that converting would be easier for me than for Tim, and that our mutual sacrifices for each other would give us even more things to share together. Actually, I had a very religious Jewish girl as my roommate in college, Nancy Aronson. She observed all the rituals that are part of her beliefs, the kosher table and the fasts and all that. I respected her ways and she mine, and we got on fine together. But we certainly were miles further apart in our religions than Tim and I, so I know I can adopt his faith and live happily in it.

Still, for these next years, golf has to dictate to a large extent how much we can be together. The chemistry of my own makeup wouldn't let me slack off until I find out just how far I can go in this game that I love so much. I've been asked which of the three big F's means the most to me: Fame, Fortune, or Fun. All three mean a lot, of course, but right now perhaps Fame has to be it because the others just go along if I achieve Fame.

In the beginning and for a long time, Fun obviously was what mattered, and Fun is still a big element in playing tournament golf because I thoroughly *enjoy* competition. And playing golf for fun will always be with me throughout my life in the years after my competitive career is over. I don't have to think about or try for Fun in golf. It surrounds me and always will.

Fortune was very important to me before the Lopezes

had any real money, and when my goal was to be able to begin repaying my parents for all the loving sacrifices they had made for me and my golf. But now that my mother is gone, and things are pretty secure in that area anyway, Fortune has taken a back seat in my mind. Between Tim's earnings and what I'm virtually sure to make in golf, even in a somewhat off-year, we ought to be all right.

So, since by this time you know I'm a very ambitious and determined woman about golf, I want to win every tournament I possibly can, and pile up a record that will give the ones who follow me something real tough to match or beat! Do you know what Roscoe once called me in an interview? "Ruthless!" He said: "The best part of her game? Well, it

Determination is my watchword

isn't any particular club. She hits them all well. It must be her mental game. Yes. There she is, all sweet and smiling, kissing her daddy before the round, then it's all business. She's got that ruthlessness. I can see her doing to the ladies what Nicklaus has done to the men."

Dad says that my secret is that I "play happy." I suspect that both Roscoe and Dad are right. But regardless of what makes me tick best, I want to go down in the golf history books if I can, and if you feel that this shows I have an embarrassingly strong ego, put the blame on my chemistry. I'd rather tag my goals as an understandable ambition.

You see, although we've had marvelous women golfers in the past, like Mickey Wright, up to now professional women's golf hasn't been important enought for sports writers to call any era "The Age of Somebody or the Other," as has happened in men's golf. In this century golf has seen "The Age of Bobby Jones," and of Ben Hogan, and of Arnold Palmer, and of Jack Nicklaus. But when they talk about the great women, the most they're apt to write is to stick in an adjective, like the "incomparable" Babe Didrikson Zaharias, or the "fabulous" Mickey Wright, or the "legendary" Patty Berg or Kathy Whitworth.

Well, I'd like to leave behind me a record that would kind of demand that golfers will think of it as "The Age of Nancy Lopez." It may be too much to hope for. It may be too much to expect. It may be beyond my reach.

But it's not too much to shoot for!